A
Body
Knows

Melanie A. May

A
Body
Knows

A
Theopoetics
of Death
and
Resurrection

CONTINUUM · NEW YORK

1995
The Continuum Publishing Company
370 Lexington Avenue, New York, NY 10017

Printed in the United States of America

Library of Congress Cataloging-in-Publication Data

May, Melanie A.
    A body knows : a theopoetics of death and resurrection / Melanie
A. May.
        p.   cm.
    Includes bibliographical references and index.
    ISBN 0-8264-0849-4 (hardcover : alk. paper)
    1. Feminist theology.   2. Body, Human—religious aspects–
–Christianity.   3. Death—Religious aspects—Christianity.
4. resurrection.   I. Title.
BT83.55.M28   1995
236′.1—dc20   95–16484
                                                                    CIP

For Bren

and

In Memoriam
Arlene Virginia Ringgold May

Visitation

Each woman listens.
Each speaks:
Ah! the life within you, within me—
    a new revelation:
    God's saving love
    impregnates the universe
    in woman . . .
    joy . . .
    Magnificat!
    Again today
    women tell their
    stories to each other—
    magnificat!
Listen sisters, listen brothers,
A new outpouring.
This time:
resurrection!

Mary Southhard*

*In *Imaging the Word: An Arts and Lectionary Resource,* Vol. 1, eds. Kenneth T. Lawrence, Jann Cather Weaver, Roger Wedell (Cleveland, Ohio: United Church Press, 1994), p. 88.

Contents

Acknowledgments

*I*f I were to call the roll of family members and friends and colleagues who have played a part in the making of this book, it would be unending. As the following pages attest, I have been and am held in life and blessed beyond measure by many persons, near and far.

I nonetheless want to name some of those to whom I am especially grateful. It was during a weekend of conversation with Roberta C. Bondi that I believe this book began to stir in me. Sharon Thornton has time and time again reflected my writing back to me in ways that have clarified my thoughts and nurtured confidence to continue. Gail Ricciuti read several chapters of an earlier manuscript, and asked for more. Members of the Friday morning breakfast (i.e., philosophy) group and of the Tuesday morning Bible study group, both in Rochester's 19th Ward where I live—Steve Horstman, Susan Kaufman, Pamela Kleiner, Adrienne Kllc, Diane Ragsdale, Maribelle Reiss, Carleen Wilenius—have loved me just as I am. President James Evans, Jr., and Dean William Herzog II, of The Divinity School here in Rochester, have offered unswerving support for my work, as have numerous faculty and student colleagues.

My father, Russell J. May, has affirmed me, and my work, in many ways through the years. Without his wisdom and his love I cannot imagine having written this book. I am grateful to my siblings and their spouses, to my nephews and nieces—Gregory and Anna, and Julia May; Jonathan and Allison, and Jessica May; Christopher and Lisa, Nathan and Thomas, Moran—for unfailingly being family. I dedicate this book to the memory of my mother, Arlene Virginia Ringgold May. Her courage and her integrity are gifts for which I will always be grateful.

I would like to thank my editor, Frank Oveis, for his faith in this book and for his skill in seeing it to publication. The steadfast support of Norman Hjelm, my friend and Faith and Order colleague, as well as consultant to Continuum Publishing, has been and continues to be a gift of grace in my life and to my work. To Ellen P. Smith, who wielded the computer in ways I cannot, always with high hilarity, I am also grateful.

Finally, and foremost, I thank Brenda Meehan, my most cherished critic and my life companion. With Bren I know love's dwelling place is "joy of heaven, to earth come down."

Introduction

> Revelation is not a development of our religious
> ideas but their continuous conversion. . . . It is
> revolutionary since it makes a new beginning
> and puts an end to the old development; it is
> permanent revolution since it can never come to
> an end in time in such a way that an irrefragable
> knowledge about God become the possession of
> an individual or group. Life in the presence of
> revelation in this respect as in all others is not
> lived before or after but in the midst of a great
> revolution.
>
> *H. Richard Niebuhr*[1]

> The text of God's revelation was, is, and will be
> written in our bodies and our peoples' everyday
> struggle for survival and liberation. . . . The lo-
> cation of God's revelation is in our life itself.
>
> *Chung Hyun Kyung*[2]

*I*t has taken me many years to be remotely ready to write
this book. Even now, I reckon readiness is a precarious,
proximate reality. I reckon this is so especially now, for as I
begin to write what my body knows of death and resurrection
my mother is dying. Her body—vibrant and vigorous, verbally
and viscerally—was the first body I knew. Now, beset by a

cancerous brain tumor eight years ago and by consequent strokes since, her body is bare-bones inert. Her skin is stretched over her skeleton, top to toe. But her eyes are more and more piercing as they sink deeper and deeper into her skull.

As I sit by her bed, I imagine an early interaction between her body and mine is recapitulated. I look into her eyes for a sign of recognition, a sign I imagine must have passed from her eyes to mine as she cradled me. But this is now no longer an exchange between mother and infant. I am the living, keeping watch with the dying; she is the dying watching me, the living. It is not the beginning but the end of recognition.

I wait for her to die. My breath bated as her breath is ragged, rattly. My grief is gagged by the sacrality of silence all around. Though tenaciously present, she is also already absent. Barely breathing. My awareness of her absent presence—body, mind, and spirit—accentuates the personal point of entry I wish to pursue in these pages.

Experiences of a lifetime have prepared me to write in this way. It nonetheless remains a challenge to relinquish the relentless requirements of razor-sharp ratiocination that characterized my years of formal theological training. I still ache as I struggle to stitch flesh and blood sensibilities onto the apparent self-sufficiency of scholarship. I am still mending my own alienated choice to dissociate logic from life that I thought was the ticket to academic achievement.

In and through this wrestling, I have become a believer. I believe I am called more than ever to tell the stories of my life—what has happened to me in my family and communities and churches, what the forms of my bondage have been, how I know what I know, how I have kept and am keeping hope alive, how I am able to lift my voice and sing sweet freedom's song, the ways in which my eyes were opened, my ears unstopped and what I see, what I hear—all the while discerning and distinguishing contingency from the features of a new course to be charted as these features appear fragmentlike along the way.

I believe it is particularly important, here and now, to talk about death and resurrection. Death is at once too rampant and too random, too romanticized and too remote. Resurrection has been terribly tamed or relegated as one more relic of a religious worldview long since worn out. Too many of us are dead while we breathe: dead to feeling, to imagination, to truth telling. Too many of us live satisfied with a shallow seriousness—sanguine or sober—since we assume what we now know is all there will be. I write to awaken myself, and others, to an awareness of death as integral to life, to awaken us to the joy of resurrection, that is, to new life abundant.

More particularly, I write about death and resurrection because my personal encounters with these realities have been most formative of my theological thinking. This wisdom wrested from blood and bones and marrow has been hard won. I have experienced my body more as betrayer than as friend. On more than one occasion death has been much more than metaphor, while resurrection was altogether a whistle in the dark. No wonder I reckon my readiness to write this book to be a precarious, proximate reality.

Still stuttering, I continue this introduction by recounting and reflecting on three experiences that craft the contours of what my body knows of death and resurrection.

The first of these experiences is threaded throughout the early years of my childhood. During these years, the highlight of many summers was a week spent with my Grandfather and Grandmother May. Their white frame farm house was set atop a knoll amid the hollows tumbling among and around West Virginia hills. Many memories of those times travel with me through the years, much as the well-worn suitcase I packed in the Shenandoah Valley of Virginia and lugged across the Civil War–drawn border. I smell the small room above the kitchen where an unruly symphony of whippoorwills, screech owls, and bobwhites accompanied my sleep. I see Granddaddy perched on a cane-bottom chair angled against the porch siding, surveying shadows that winded their way across the hay fields, barn, sheds, and house.

Most graphically, in my heart's eye, I see Grandma, planted amid the corn stalks and bean poles and red ripening tomatoes sprawling over the plot of ground where sunlight generously shone through the hollows and ridges of those hills. A broad-brimmed straw hat is string-tied under her sturdy chin. Her hoe is in her hand. I imagine it is a staff and she is leading a band of people instead of leaning into patches of persistent weeds. Grandma May. On her lips I first heard, "A body knows."

Schooled on philosophical suppositions that privilege the mind and on theology crafted coherently in constructionist concepts[3], it has taken me many years to recognize and retrieve the theological wisdom of my Grandmother May's words. A body knows. In those early years I did not really hear her. My life, my body, and my knowledge were held hostage to messages—sublime and searing—permeating the cultural and religious scripts and streams into which I was born. Even before I had read a page of Augustine or Aquinas, Descartes or Freud, I had learned my body was to be kept clean and controlled and in check. And I had learned because my body was to be a woman's body it was to be watched and worn with particular decorum. Being energetic and enthusiastic—really rambunctious—as a farm girl, being strong and nearly six feet tall already as an early adolescent, I found these lessons were trying at best.

These lessons were also bewildering. My Grandmother May's body, for example, seemed an exception. Her arms and legs and back worked as hard as or harder than those of any man I met, while the exquisitely wrought bones of her wrists and ankles and cheeks announced womanliness according to any cultural code considered. And as she hoed and baked and washed and minded her grandchildren, I did not sense she suffered the subjugation I subsequently studied in analyses of women as mothers or domestic members of families and communities. She moved with an authority all her own outside and inside the house, active in arenas I later learned were delineated as public and private.[4] Above all, I was aware she was esteemed by neighbors nestled in hollows and along ridges as a woman who would respond with her herbs or her heart when a body was ailing or aggrieved. They knew she knew, a body knows.

I do not mean to idealize my Grandmother May's life. But neither do I wonder what she would have done had she lived with what I have assumed to be more choice relative to my body. Instead I wonder how as I grew I forgot what she embodied, how as I grew I ignored what my body knew and knows. I wonder how I, long a shirtless resister of convention and propriety, surrendered my body to be what Michel Foucault has aptly called a site of social control.[5]

A second experience occurred at the time of my M.Div. graduation at Harvard Divinity School. I was elected by my class in early April to deliver the student baccalaureate address. Being conscientious—frankly compulsive—that very evening I diligently set out to determine what might be appropriate words for the occasion. A recent perusal of those jottings reveals the following themes: encouragement to enact ideas we had shaped during our years as students; strength to build a new order in the midst of a world order already apparently falling apart, etc.

But a ruptured disk and back surgery and weeks of recuperation before commencement changed my perspective considerably. Consequently, my speech was not words about anticipated achievements. I could no longer assume that simply because we had honed our critical capacities and polished our powers of articulation we would sally forth to save the world.

My changed perspective testified not to apathy or bitterness or cynicism or despair in the face of human impotence or life's tragedy. I did not conclude we were best counseled to resign ourselves to an inexorable momentum by which the world and we with it would inevitably be swept along or away. My changed perspective was a gesture of grace in the face of life's mystery, the mystery that grief and ecstasy, as dying and rising, are always mingled moments.

I learned these mingled moments are moments of sensibility that embodied life is limited life, and that according to biblical narratives those whom God chose as leaders were those aware of their limits. I also learned that to live without an awareness of my limits I would languish, a prisoner to my preoccupation with being perfect, being without failure or flaw. I began to see that thus imprisoned I forfeited my freedom to receive new life abundant, which is always a gift.

Still I struggled. I strained against the limits about which my body was so articulate, so wise. By now a doctoral student at Harvard, I clothed and exercised and fed, but did not live in my body. I assumed its abilities were at my mind's beck and call. I presumed its aches and pains were annoyances, or attestations to single-minded scholarly achievement. My body's rhythms and reckonings, its delights and desires, were a foreign language. I tied my native tongue.

The third experience occurred three years later when I had to reckon that what I thought was my fear of finitude was fear of life. Late one night, after a two-month hospitalization, I, along with my doctors, thought I was dying. I felt my body my self slip away, head first, into a yawning tunnel, endlessly open.

Since that night, I have countenanced the fact that I am not merely finite. I am mortal. Accordingly, I have learned I do not merely have a body. I am my body.

These acknowledgments announced my struggle against the traditions into which I was born, traditions that associate women with the body, more specifically with the body's "natural," i.e., sexual, reproductive, domestic, functions. Suckled on these streams of thought, I learned to try to transcend my body, lest I be sullied by its consequently inherent corruptibility and, in the company of centuries of women, be scapegoated as a sinner.

Taking tortuous, tortoise-style steps, I have set my sights on subversion. As I do so, I figure my fear of being fully alive, my fear of new life abundant is founded in the transitoriness of life itself, a fear fueled by the traditions into which I was born. These traditions did not and do not tolerate the ambiguity attendant to the mysterious and often tragic cycle of birth and death at the heart of life itself. Trying to transcend the body, and accordingly women, these traditions have tried to transcend finitude and, most of all, mortality.[6]

Subversion has for me meant a struggle to affirm life *is* transitory, to affirm life's character *is* change, even if often in ways I would not choose. Indeed, to be alive is *precisely* to change. I struggle, therefore, to *affirm* what I can "impute . . . to no cause, nor call . . . by any name."[7] I wrestle with the reckoning that the world I know will be at risk if I am altogether alive as I breathe, with the reckoning that there are no promises about hurt and longing, if I awaken to new life abundant. I thereby "practice resurrection."[8]

I *practice* resurrection, for God, who came to be with us in the One who went to the cross, went down to hell, and *then* to glory, is the God of surprises by human reckoning. Amid the mysterious and often tragic mingling of grief and ecstasy, dying and rising, God brings down the mighty and lifts up the lowly. God's surprises are most often more unsettling than settling reversals of the road on which we have set out. The more I have to lose the harder it may be to be alive, to let go what is, to leave the predictable "as a sign to mark the false trail,"[9] and thereby to awaken to new life abundant.

So I still stutter into speech by way of this personal point of entry. I practice but I do not celebrate resurrection. For I feel as if it is Holy Saturday. This day, the day between Jesus' crucifixion on Good Friday and Jesus' resurrection on Easter Sunday, is a day about which the Gospels are silent. I agree with Hans Urs von Balthasar, who notes this silence and thinks it is appropriate, since we would otherwise be tempted to tell ourselves death is "a partial event."[10] It is true that for most of my life I have skipped from Good Friday blithely across the abyss of Holy Saturday to Easter Sunday. After all, I have known the story has a happy ending.

But during the first Easter Sunday worship service after my breast cancer diagnosis, when we sang "Where, O death, is now thy sting?" I knew the exact spot death still stung my body! Since that Easter Sunday, Holy Saturday has been a hallowed space for my mortal body. I want, as I write, to stand in this space, thereby to straddle—not settle or subdue—these tensive days of drama. For I know I cannot celebrate resurrection without descending to the dead, since practicing means making "more tracks than necessary, some in the wrong direction."[11]

The following chapters articulate the flesh and blood and bones of this conviction. In distinction from my former theological work,[12] herein "body" is neither an image nor a symbol Christologically or ecclesiologically rendered. Herein "body" is made of mud and the wild holiness of wind.[13] And so I want to wrestle more fiercely than I ever have Paul's rhetorical question to the Christians at Corinth: "do you not know that your body is a temple of the Holy Spirit within you?" (I Cor. 6:19, NRSV) So honoring my body, I seek to set free its theological knowledge, its theological wisdom. Each chapter therefore begins with an account of one of my encounters with death—anticipating resurrection to new life abundant—and explores the theological knowledge thereby enunciated.

I deepen my account of my near-death experience, which was accompanied by an epiphany-like experience of being in light, in chapter 1. These experiences, by teaching me to fear death in life more than death itself, loosened my hold on the life I had been leading, and subsequently severed the no longer life-giving connective tissue that had bound me to family and church and community as I had known them. Indeed, I became acutely aware that too many things that had bound me to others and to the earth had been betrayed.

Consequently, these experiences led me to explore new and life-giving forms of human connection, in relation to my family and community, but especially with reference to what it means to be the church today. This exploration is timely, for so many churches in the United States are trying to salvage and shore up what has been, and in so doing are forfeiting life in the risen Christ. I seek instead to pay attention to what Leonardo Boff has referred to as "the new experiences of church in our midst"[14] as I articulate a new and concrete ecclesial vision.

In chapter 2, I reflect on the ways a potentially life-threatening diagnosis of breast cancer coupled my lessons about fear of life with lessons about fear of love. My body's articulation was breathtakingly astute. My breast catalyzed a crisis of nurturance. Not until then could I countenance the love lost in my life. Love was lost, but not because I was not loved. I grew up embraced by the generous and gracious love of my parents and siblings, my grandparents and extended family, my friends, lovers, and church community. Still, lessons about long-suffering, self-sacrificial, love suffuse the radical reformation tradition in which I was formed.[15] Love was lost because the sacrificial—the selfless—love I learned was attended by an unholy hatred of my self, a self-hatred that blinded me to the ways I was well loved by others. Audre Lorde was altogether right when she said: "I have to learn to love myself before I can love you or accept your loving. You have to learn to love yourself before you can love me or accept my loving. Know we are worthy of touch before we can reach out for each other."[16]

I first made this wrenching acknowledgment about love lost during the time I was undergoing radiation therapy, following a lumpectomy and a lymph-node dissection. So many people poured out so much love. Since then, I have struggled not only to understand, but to learn the lessons of love lost. In chapter 2, I reflect on what I have learned with particular reference to the ways in which these lessons have profoundly informed my work as an ecumenical theologian.

I believe, this is to say, that the preoccupation with unity in terms of acceptable limits of diversity, even in terms of an agreement that advances uniformity, misses the heart of the biblical call to hospitality. This call is a call to extend hospitality to those we believe to be unlovable as well as lovable, hospitality to the stranger in our own midst and the stranger by whom we are met outside the fences of our fear. Even more uncomfortably, this is a call to *accept* the hospitality offered by the stranger, to sit as a guest at the stranger's table.

Chapter 3 is informed by a diagnosis of manic depression in my thirty-ninth year. Even setting aside the destructive social stigma attached to this diagnosis, manic depression is a lethal disease if not properly treated. I was at once relieved and enraged that this diagnostic clarity came after so many years of suffering more and more severe mood swings, swings I thought were signs of moral failure.

Facing this diagnosis, taking medication to normalize my brain's neurotransmitters together with working in therapy, has been a purifying fire, burning away the burden of moral culpability along with the acidity of societal judgment. I am present to my self and to others as I have not heretofore been. I live with a sense of my own authority—this is to say, no longer captive to and constrained by external expectations—as I have not before. Knowing what my body knows about manic depression relative to presence and authority, I recast my perspective on the practice of ministry in these regards.

In chapter 4, I speak about truth telling, which I still believe sets free. I do so as I write about being lesbian in death-dealing homophobic churches and societies worldwide. I write out of the hope about which James Baldwin wrote. "Revealing one's nakedness . . . is, really, our only human hope,"[17] he said.

Out of this clarity of my conviction that truth telling is revelatory, I explore the practice of preaching as becoming the flesh of one's words, as bearing witness in one's body to the Good News—news always arriving from another shore—proclaiming what is is not what will be, affirming God is indeed the God of radical and risky reversals. In short and in sum, I write to keep alive hope, hope that what now is will give way to what will be upon this earth.

Finally, in chapter 5, I reflect on the methodological implications of what my body knows as written in chapters 1 through 4, by articulating theology as doxology. I do not hereby mean to suggest that it is plausible or possible simply to start, or finish, the theological task with "God," as if God were immediately accessible to me or to any of us. In this regard, my theological training with Gordon Kaufman at Harvard Divinity School, who argues that theology is an activity of "imaginative construction,"[18] remains formative. I agree with his assertion that all my words to or about God are *my* words: always inadequate and always inviting my self-conscious responsibility. To say theology is doxology is, however, also to say doxology—praise giving or thanksgiving—is itself theology. I thereby assert that theology proper is not only second-order, constructionist discourse, but also the lively, multivalent language spoken face-to-face with the mystery of birth and death and resurrection that is life.

To say theology is doxology also affirms my experience and women's experience to be a source of theological knowledge. More specifically, as the chapters introduced above attest, I believe what our bodies know is a life-giving source of our knowledge of God.[19] As Naomi Goldenberg puts it: "In the beginning was definitely not the Word. . . . It is flesh that makes the words."[20]

This epistemological point is prefaced by the shared conviction that women's experience has too often been absent in or abused by the Christian theological tradition. More profoundly, this epistemological point proclaims my confession that I am created to be doxology, i.e., to "glorify God in [my] body" (I Cor. 6:20, NRSV). I am created as a mortal body to be thanksgiving, and so beholding the glory of God to be "changed into the same image from glory to glory" (II Cor. 3: 18, KJV).

I know that the affirmation of *imago Dei* has been ambiguously interpreted throughout the centuries of the Christian tradition. The *imago Dei* has been spiritualized or rendered rationally, even though early theologians such as Irenaeus were clear that human beings—body and soul—are created in God's image. Taken spiritually or rendered rationally, women have accordingly and traditionally been excluded from the affirmation of *imago Dei*, except as they are under the headship of men. I nonetheless appeal to the affirmation of *imago Dei* as I articulate theology as doxology in order to assert, together with Elizabeth A. Johnson,[21] that the glory of God is at risk as long as any woman, or any man, is at risk of diminishment or destruction. The doxological perspective I proclaim, this is to say, is a hymn to the sacrality of moral bodies and of earthly life, created to glorify and to bear witness to the source and sustainer of being who at once incarnates and is beyond all our words.

Accordingly, I punctuate these chapters with my poetry. I do so not only because my earliest expressions of what my body knows of death and resurrection were poetic. More profoundly, poetry, in the words of Audre Lorde, is "the way we help give name to the nameless so it can be thought."[22] It is in this sense I write a theopoetics, since I am convinced, as was Amos Wilder: "Old words do not reach across the new gulfs."[23]

I also write a theopoetics in the sense in which Christine Downing writes "a poetics of gender" in her book, *Women's Mysteries: Toward a Poetics of Gender.*[24] "To accept gender as *made*," writes Downing, "as a *poesis*, means seeing it as always still in the process of being made and remade. . . . As poets of gender, we can engage in the exploration of alternative perspectives and perhaps even in the creation of new ones.[25] Herein, this is to say, I intend to articulate alternative perspectives or create new perspectives on the church, ecumenism, ministry, preaching, and the doing of theology. My articulation is also poetic inasmuch as these alternative or new perspectives are not conceptually complete or systematically settled. As I write I invite others to participate in what I believe to be an ongoing process of naming, clarifying, and loosing again: to honor *poesis* as making and remaking without ceasing.

Finally, I write amid poetic pronunciation to affirm that there is theological wisdom—face-to-face with mystery and tangled in ambiguity—that cannot otherwise be conveyed.[26]

What I write is an expansion and extension of the experiential traditions of theological knowledge.[27] In so doing, I not only underscore the question as to whose experience counts as a source for theology. What counts as theological knowledge and how we know are also put into question, since the transfiguration of our minds, as surely as the resurrection of our bodies, is at stake. What is finally at stake is at once honoring our individual distinctions and birthing new forms of life-giving connection to one another, to all mortal and earthly creation, to the glory of God.

This theological testament to what my body knows is an act of resistance against the terror and tyranny—and the inarticulate internalized grief and rage that sets the selves we become in order to survive against our own best selves—that chokes our voices and cuts us off from what our bodies know. This act of resistance is also an act of trespass. Believing death is not an end but a new beginning, herein I dare to disregard the boundaries that have defined academic disciplines and Christianity and churches and families . . . and more.

So here on Holy Saturday, straddling tensive days of drama, I stand on this threshold to write in solidarity with all mortal and earthly bodies—scarred and sacred, broken and blessed—and to the glory of God our creator. As I write I wrestle with my anguished question: how have I forgotten my mortal body, my female body, which is my "first body of knowledge,"[28] is created to glorify God and to be "changed into the same image from glory to glory" (II Cor. 3:18, KJV)?

In the end, my body knows, there is no answer, only an end. Still, I will not let go. Even now, as I herein descend to the dead, I expect the unexpected. Especially now, because by most medical reckonings my mother should already be among the dead. But she is still in the land of the living. The mysterious mingling of dying and rising made flesh of my flesh. Awakened to this mysterious mingling, as I write I keep vigil with my mother. Keeping vigil, I am prepared to be astonished, knowing I practice resurrection.

One

Living in the Light

> . . . I had an epiphany, that the light we encounter on the road of death is our being in the act of coming home to itself. I understood that light is our natural state, but . . . we must be born and die many times to reach the light.[1]

*F*aces and figures of a lifetime danced before my eyes. One by one, then all together, they danced out over a precipice I could barely perceive. As familiar faces and figures fell away in front of me, I floated headfirst into a tunnel opening behind me. The tunnel was a yawning mouth. The tunnel was arms ready to receive and rock my beleaguered, broken body.

This was the night I thought I was going to die. My doctor thought so too. Nurses moved in and out of my room, keeping worried watch.

This night was in March 1982 and I had already been in the hospital nearly two months. I was admitted in mid-January for severe back pain. Back pain in my case was not a casual matter. In the spring of 1979 I had had a ruptured disk surgically removed. Now my doctor suspected another disk had weakened to the point of rupture.

An excruciating—dare I say electrifying?—diagnostic test, the myelogram, was inconclusive. Consequently a conservative regimen of bed rest, muscle relaxers, and traction was prescribed and pursued. At the end of the first month I was better, but I still could not walk without considerable pain. At this point, after a number of consultations, I chose to add another treatment to those already tried: an epidural nerve block that would numb my muscles cramped in protective protest and so break the circuit of pain.

It worked. In a day or two the pain had substantially subsided and I was able to walk again. I was discharged from the hospital shortly thereafter.

When I was discharged I had a low-grade fever for which no one could account but about which no one was worried. Within three days I was paralyzed from the point the nerve block had been injected downward. And I was in awful agony. I felt as if I were being electrocuted, so sheer were the charges catching and bating my breath.

I returned to the hospital in an ambulance and lay in the emergency room all day. Since my diagnosis was assumed to be orthopedic I was not high on the emergency room hierarchy of need. My dear friend Diana Eck stood by me and told me Hindu myths, recited Hindu prayers, and held my hand.

Finally, in the early evening, I was taken to the orthopedic floor and put to bed. A friend, Dr. Joseph Martin, Chief of Neurology and at that time Acting Director of Massachusetts General Hospital, happened to have heard I had been readmitted and so stopped by on his way home. He took one look at me, undertook a neurological examination, and spent the night in the hospital scheduling a battery of diagnostic tests for the following morning.

I awakened to see seven or so neurologists, who happened to be in town for a professional meeting, circling my bed. My heart went wild. But pain was a pacifier. I heard hushed whispers about multiple sclerosis and was still numb.

The diagnosis was transverse myelitis, meaning a transverse section of my spinal cord was severely inflamed. No wonder I felt as if I were being electrocuted! I was. At the time, Massachusetts General was one of a few hospitals to have a treatment for transverse myelitis other than the traditional treatment of steroids. Steroids could arrest but rarely reverse the paralysis. The new treatment, which I underwent five times over the next several weeks, replaced my blood plasma in order to strengthen my immune system for the fight against inflammation.

I got better. I got worse. And so it went as the weeks went. On one hand, this is typical of the disease. On another hand, I know by then my body was drifting into a deep depression that complicated the course of recovery.

And so the night I thought I was dying arrived. The pain was so excruciating that even the vibration of footfalls on the floor was virtually unbearable. As I lay there, seeing familiar faces and figures falling away, seeing and sensing my self slipping away, there suddenly surged through me the will to live. What I felt was surely what Susan Griffin described as a "roaring inside."[2] I realized I was not ready to let life go.

I cannot say why. I did not need reasons then. I am not inclined to seek such now. My response to the roaring belongs to the realm of mystery, along with ageless wondering about why we are at all anyway.

My response then and there was kinetic. My body moved without reserve to reach for the telephone receiver. Eloquence enacted. My body knew to be alive is to be connected. I do not remember dialing, but without doubt did. Within minutes Diana, and my dear friend Dorothy Austin, were with me, holding me in life. I cried, choking and coughing into their bodies circling mine. Dorothy prayed as only Dorothy can pray. I do remember a rush of presence pervading the room. Real presence.[3] I fell into a sleep as deep as death.

And very early on the morning of the next day, as I awakened, Diana and Dorothy were in the doorway of my room. I called out to them to stay where they were, got out of bed, and walked to them. We embraced. The following morning I was discharged from the hospital.

For many years this experience has been my near-death experience. I have trembled to tell it. I have imagined my self a brand snatched from the burning. Still charred and smoking.

Not until eleven years later, during the Lenten season of 1993, did I learn about the light. By then I was at the Divinity School in Rochester, New York, and was anticipating the inauguration of The Program in the Study of Women and Gender in Church and Society, together with my installation as Dean of The Program in May. I had asked Dorothy to preach on the occasion of my installation. She called to talk with me about her sermon.

The theme for the inaugural events was the theme chosen for 1993 celebrations of the midpoint of the Ecumenical Decade: Churches in Solidarity with Women, 1988–98: "Standing Together in Hope." Dorothy said as we talked that she could not preach on this theme without preaching about that afternoon eleven years earlier. "But it was night," I impatiently replied, wondering what had happened to her memory of so momentous a scene. "Yes, I know," she said, "but what I remember was that there was so much light." "What light?" I said, stupefied. "As we left that night," Dorothy recalled, "the room was filled with a great, glowing light." When I could breathe I blurted: "Why did no one tell me?" Dorothy gasped: "We thought you knew."

But I had *not* known. Suddenly my near-death experience was transfigured into an epiphany-like experience of light. A resurrection reversal. Death indeed not an ending but a new beginning.

Perhaps if I *had* known earlier I would have lapsed into an eager leap from Good Friday across the abyss of Holy Saturday to Easter Sunday. Perhaps I would not have descended to the dead and, face-to-face with death, discovered I did not fear it. Perhaps I could never have written "Blood Blessing":

> death does not do that to me
> no tentacles   no terrors
> but buoyant arms to hold
> to honor

now the everlasting erupts
these incandescent times
while I whisper
I am
the golden thread
spun of fire   soaked in flame
I shimmer as an awakening leaf
like light on lively water
and wing my way   mooncruising
to you

to testify to new meanings
to moments cast off carefree
anchored amid sun and stone
quarries hewn and holy

and so we spread ourselves
the feast
of possibility   of promise
careful of the clutch

and so I bless the blood spilled
mindful of mortality
redolent with resurrection
and you

Perhaps, this is to say, I would not have awakened to this wonder of new life abundant, blessed by cherished company and intimate connection.

As it was, I had to practice resurrection in these regards a long time. The immediate consequence of my ordeal was a severance of, at least a severe strain in, connections to family, community, and church. These connections were and are rooted in the stubborn limestone soil of the Shenandoah Valley of Virginia. Living in a lineage six generations long—the seventh is well under way—my body belongs to this earth, especially the earth of Maymont Farm near Timberville on the North Fork of the Shenandoah River. But, having been to the brink and back, I felt estranged from the people and places to which I had belonged, to which I had been connected from my childhood. My world was in rubble, I realized. And I was among those to whom Willie's grandmother, in Thulani Davis's novel *1959*, referred when she remarked: "you don't understand about life. Many things are taken from you."[4]

But I also felt betrayed. During my convalescence, which continued through the spring of 1982, I read Michel Foucault for the first time. His writings, wrought out of the Paris revolt of 1968, turned my way of seeing upside down.[5] Almost in an instant, I saw that many of the bonds by which I had been held in life were all too precisely bonds. I had been in bondage. Now seeing, with Foucault, from the perspective of the prisoner not the prison guard, the patient not the doctor, etc., I myself revolted from the regime of expectations regarding what to do and what not to do that had been the price of belonging, of being connected.

In the wake of my revolt I figured what I had thought to be my fear of death was in fact my fear of life. I feared life, now knowing in my flesh and bones and blood that many things would be taken from me. And my fear was confounded insofar as I had collaborated with my own confinement in the face of it. I had collaborated with my confinement within exclusionary walls erected to eliminate what would not be conformed, what could not be controlled.[6] Death in life indeed.

In March 1990 I articulated my death in life in a poem, "The Driest Thorn":

> heavy   heaving.
> But nary a stone's squeezings from this still
> stuck so far back in the bottom of a Virginia valley
> not even the eager revenuer in his rattly red Rambler
> would try to track or trail it:

dry-hearted.
Indeed I am a drought-resistant strain.
My story line's laced with learning not to luxuriate
in soft spring rain or soak in puddles,
putting in time toughening to the way things are:

a plea bitterly bargained.
Recently the line's unraveling.
I'm counting the cost of continuity,
along with links in the chain,
studying a sky slung without script or sign:

mute and meaningless.
the seeds I scattered in the garden
yesterday will yield growth
and brown shoots will get green
during my drag across this desert:

armed with a canteen.
Stalking the source of my sadness
where water's scarce and the sacred's silent.
Wrestling the river sprites for a secret,
likelihood impaled upon the driest thorn.

My alienation was ameliorated already in the summer of 1983. Having honored a long-standing commitment to speak at the Church of the Brethren Annual Conference in Baltimore, I went to the Valley to visit family for the first time in more than a year. When I arrived I heard that my maternal Grandmother's house had been ransacked. The house in which Grandmother Ringgold had lived until two years earlier was built by my Great, Great, Great Grandfather Jacob Miller of bricks fired in a kiln that was built alongside the bank-style barn that still stands, having survived Sheridan's Civil War raid through the Valley. The house was bulging with the artifacts of many of my ancestors.

Taking a momentary glance at the mess, I counseled my mother to hire someone to trash it, to take the rubble out and away. Thankfully, she ignored my counsel. And I spent the next two weeks sorting the stuff of lifetimes of my legacy with her. These weeks changed my life. A wrong direction diverted, as daily my body touched artifacts that articulated, and so attached me anew to the quarry from which I was hewn.

Once more my body taught me that to be alive, abundantly so, is to be connected. But not indiscriminately. My mother and I filled a lot of trash bags, eventually truck beds, as we retrieved glassware and furnishings and letters, some of which now grace my dining table, my living room and bed room, and are the makings of a future writing project: a novel whose texture will be woven of fifty years worth of my Great Great Aunt Sally's letters from Denver to her sister, my Great Grandmother, who stayed in the Valley.

It was this tactile experience, along with my inability, indeed unwillingness, to countenance a continuance of academic life— switching sides of the desk, as I put it at the time—that prepared me to accept an appointment to the national staff of the Church of the Brethren, in the Chicago suburb of Elgin on the Fox River. I served in several positions, specifically Director of Program for Women, Ecumenical Officer, and Associate General Secretary for Human Resources, for tenures of varying lengths over a period of six years. I longed for the theological words I had written to become flesh. I imagined incarnation.

The beginning of my tenure on national staff was the beginning of a time of turmoil for churches in the United States. Within a couple of years, Wade Clark Roof and William McKinney set the initial terms of ongoing talk about shifting demographics and definitions of American religious communities, particularly documenting the decline of those communities considered to constitute the mainline religious establishment.[7] Roof and McKinney were joined by Robert Wuthnow, who analyzed the decline of denominationalism, and argued that the contours of a deepening conservative/liberal chasm ran within rather than across these traditional lines defining American church life.[8]

I was not, nor am I, among the throngs mourning the much-discussed disestablishment of so-called mainline Protestant churches in the United States. What I mourned then and still mourn today is the fear by which churches are motivated as the forms of church we have known are dying. I mourn as I see churches building higher walls rather than breaking down walls that have divided and excluded God's people for decades and centuries. As I learned while sorting stuff in my Grandmother's house, I believe that the rubble of wrecked walls can begin to clear a way to resurrection life.

My perspective on what was and is happening in American church life no doubt bears the mark of my early formation in a church considered to be among the marginal relative to the mainline. I have, therefore, been and continue to be more compelled by the thinking of R. Laurence Moore and Nathan Hatch about American religious culture than by that of Roof and McKinney and Wuthnow. R. Laurence Moore, in his *Religious Outsiders and the Making of Americans*, argues not only that contemporary, and conventional, distinctions between the religious "mainstream" and the "marginal" are more strategic than substantiated creations of historians. Moore also calls the cause for current lament into question as he argues against past scholarship: "It is impossible to locate a period of American history when so-called small sects were not growing at a faster clip than denominations then viewed as large and stable."[9]

Hatch reinforces Moore's perspective as he reassesses the character of American Christianity in the era of the young republic. Moreover, his argument that the plethora of popular religious movements testifies to a pervasive and ongoing bent toward decentralization of power, toward democratization, precisely in the face of established churches' claims to knowledge and power,[10] opened my eyes to the way in which the contemporary crisis is a spiritual crisis. Although most so-called mainline churches have responded to dwindling membership and money by shoring up bureaucratic structures, as if structural change could stem the tide, Hatch's historical analysis makes it clear to me that in this crisis, as in many others, "the people know what to do, before the leaders."[11] And, although I know that many members of churches in this country are captive to the fear catalyzed by the dying of what we have known as church, are afraid to let go and greet life abundant, I believe there are people ready and willing to walk—indeed, are already walking—out of the tombs wherein we hide in fear to follow the risen Christ who goes on ahead.

This reflection on shifting religious culture in this country sent me to a rereading of H. R. Niebuhr's *The Social Sources of Denominationalism*. While there is more sociocultural similarity among and between denominations now than when Niebuhr wrote in the late 1920s—except for the fact that most churches are still racially separatist and Sunday morning is the most racially segregated time of the week across the country—I believe his insight into what he called "the evil of denominationalism" is as pertinent relative to today's crisis as it was then. For from Niebuhr's perspective, beyond the failure of the churches "to transcend the social conditions which fashion them into caste-organizations,"[12] i.e., their failure to transcend divisiveness and exclusivity, "the evil of denominationalism" is rooted in the churches' failure "to resist the temptation of making their own self-preservation and extension the primary object of their endeavor."[13] Niebuhr spoke of "the evil of denominationalism" as "the moral failure of Christianity,"[14] since he was convinced denominationalism was a sign that the world has succeeded in shaping the body of Christ into but one among the secular organizations, most of which are members-only clubs of the likeminded.[15]

Niebuhr is much more unqualified in his critique of "sects" than I am inclined to be, since the quarry from which I was hewn has for much of its history understood itself as and been understood to be a "sect."[16] Although I agree with Niebuhr's argument that "sects" have contributed to contemporary cultural alienation, I also see "sects" in light of what Niebuhr calls "the creative center of movements of the Spirit which have penetrated the world."[17] The difference between my point of view and Niebuhr's may be indicated by my change of his singular "center" to plural "centers."

This is to say, I think far too few theologians or church and ecumenical leaders have yet been honest enough about the contemporary movement of the Spirit to create new faces and forms of the church. Brazilian theologian Leonardo Boff puts this point this way: "If we are to develop a new ecclesiology, we shall need more than just theological perspicacity and historico-dogmatic erudition. We must fact the new experiences of church in our midst."[18] Too many of us have not heard or taken to heart the Good News heralded to us in our day as to the women on the first Easter. The women went into the tomb, not fearing to descend to the dead, and there, according to Luke's account, they heard the news: "Why do you look for the living among the dead? He is not here, but has risen" (Luke 24:5b, NRSV).

According to Mark's account, then and there terror seized the women. We are told "they said nothing to anyone, for they were afraid" (Mark 16:8b, NRSV). I think it is appropriate that Mark's account ends with the women's flight. I think it is appropriate that the denouement of the story is still pending. For I believe the making of an ending is an everlasting matter in which we are all called to participate.[19]

I believe this to be so since I believe that Jesus' death was a tragic and unnecessary act of violence perpetrated by leaders of the religious establishment of his day, who were as fearful as most religious leaders of our day. His suffering and death, therefore, were and are not as such salvific.[20] The cross thus stands as a sign of his courageous and faithful life: an attestation to the love that casts out fear and to the truth that sets free.[21] Accordingly, I believe that the body of the risen Christ is made manifest whenever and wherever people gather to bear witness to this loving, truth-telling way of life, to incarnate a common life into which all are welcomed as members who participate as prophetic witnesses in a world no less violent than Jesus'.

So I still imagine incarnation. But I do not do so naively. My tenure on the Church of the Brethren national staff ended, at least in part, in the wake of several charges of sexual harassment came to me for disposition in my office as Associate General Secretary of Human Resources. I was not one of the women who was first abused and who finally had the courage to advance charges. But I swiftly became aware that abuse is never satisfied until it has snared all who are anywhere around. I was not spared. And so my eyes were opened to ancient patterns of abuse—my collaboration with confinement and my consequent death in life—patterns I now named the tyranny[22] of community. An awful revelation. And yet also a relief to be aware, to be awakened.

My steps toward healing were steps to take back—once again—the life I thought I owed the church. I took a step by taking back the words of the hymn—"O Love That Wilt Not Let Me Go"[23]—I chose to sing when I was ordained to the ministry in 1984, saying: if this be love, I let it go. I took another step by tampering with the words of another hymn— "Take My Life and Let It Be"[24]—sown into my body's sinew, saying: my life . . . let it be! So coming to my senses I am coming home to myself. Being willing to let go what was no longer life-giving, I am awakening to life abundant.

Again, I am also not naive about the violence to which many new, popular religious movements are giving rise, as Mark Juergensmeyer, for example, documents all too well in his *The New Cold War? Religious Nationalism Confronts the Secular State.*[25] Juergensmeyer cites Harriet Crabtree's Harvard doctoral dissertation, in which she finds the "model of warfare" to be a prominent image articulated in hymns, tracts, and sermons of some "popular theologies" of contemporary Protestant Christianity. Citing preacher and religious writer, Arthur Wallis, Crabtree claims the image of warfare in these "popular theologies" is not "a metaphor or a figure of speech" but a "literal fact."[26]

Still, I see signs of Christ's risen body—what I name new ecclesial realities[27]—all around the world. Among these signs, these realities, are base communities throughout Latin America and in the Philippines,[28] African independent churches,[29] house churches or small groups in the United States,[30] women's communities throughout Asia,[31] Women-Church communities among Protestant as well as Roman Catholic women across the United States,[32] etc. Christ is risen, indeed!

I know the perils of pointing to characteristics that are common to such vastly variegated communities. I also know the characteristics I see in these communities are no doubt akin to ecclesiological expressions of the radical reformation tradition I still cherish. So saying, I nonetheless venture to name two characteristics I believe to be common to these signs of Christ's risen body, to these new ecclesial realities.

The first characteristic is that the people who are committed to these communities are committed to mending the breach between word and flesh,[33] between worship and public witness, between justice seeking and doxology, by *being* witnesses to the new creation promised and already present in Christ. Whether by forming economic cooperatives or celebrating freshly written liturgies or advocating ecclesial or political transformation, or being profoundly present in one another's lives, these communities are giving birth to new forms of human connection in an age of alienation.

A second characteristic is the declaration—in word and deed—that the people *are* the church. In the twentieth century, this declaration is at least as old as the Second Vatican Council.[34] It is as new as each and every community that attests in its body to Jesus' words to the disciples: "Truly I tell you, whatever you bind on earth will be bound in heaven, and whatever you loose on earth will be loosed in heaven" (Matt. 18:18, NRSV). Being a Protestant, a radical reformation Protestant no less, this has not been a verse I have often cited! This verse has traditionally been interpreted in light of a preceding verse in Matthew 16, the verse taken by Roman Catholics to be the foundation of papal authority: "you are Peter, and on this rock I will build my church, and the gates of Hades will not prevail against it. I will give you the keys of the kingdom of heaven, and whatever you bind on earth will be bound in heaven, and whatever you loose on earth will be loosed in heaven" (Matt. 16:18–19, NRSV).

But recently I have read Matthew 18:18 with new eyes as I read it with Walbert Buhlmann, who believes:

> This latter logion appears as part of the "community rule," in which Jesus apprises the community, or the communities, even small groups, indeed, families as domestic churches, of their full responsibility to decide their daily questions independently, in good conscience, and in the Holy Spirit. . . . All who believe in Jesus, and who belong to his community, should be not simply passive beneficiaries, but active administrators, of the power of binding and loosing.[35]

Binding and loosing is biblical language for what I write about in language of connecting and letting go.

Binding and loosing, as connecting and letting go, is a rhythm of reckoning what is life-giving and what is death-dealing. This is a rhythm that insists I live with my own sense of authority, that insists I live unbound by the external expectations erected as confinement in earlier times of my life. And so this rhythm has been and is the heartbeat of my life, most profoundly since the night I nearly, but did not, let life go, since the night my body knew and articulated the truth that to be alive is to be connected.

I believe this rhythm is also constitutive of the church as the risen body of Christ. I believe this to be so not only because I believe that what we know to be church dies and rises to new life as long as the church is Christ's risen body rather than a whited sepulchre testifying to fear. I also believe this rhythm is constitutive of the church because the church as the risen body of Christ is always gathering and dispersing. The church, this is to say, is a gathering of those who together incarnate the one in whose name we gather. The church is also always dispersing, as its members are again and again being sent into the world to bear witness to the Good News of new and liberating life abundant for all.

But my vision of the church is as trinitarian as it is Christological. I believe the church is first and finally a communion of persons,[36] not a bureaucratic institution, a denomination, or a voluntary association. The church is a communion of persons who participate, by the grace of the Holy Spirit, in the very life of God. And as participants in the very life of God, all are "changed into the same image from glory to glory" (II Cor. 3:18, KJV).

So saying, I turn to the story of the Transfiguration. According to Matthew's account, high up on a mountain, Jesus was transfigured before Peter, James, and John: "and his face did shine as the sun, and his raiment was white as the light" (Matt. 17:2, KJV). According to Orthodox theology, this is not a story of the divine appearing to the human, of the creator appearing to the creature. It is rather a story of the human, the creaturely, becoming a participant in divine glory.[37] Accordingly, it is, for me, a story of the light. It is the story of an epiphany—an appearance—of the life abundant in which we are all created to participate. Living in the light, bearing witness in our bodies—individual and corporate—to the shining brightness, is the church's calling as well as its constitution. For, as our *being* together is an icon of the very life of God, we are *active* cocreators with God of a new way of being, a way of being woven as each and every one assumes the authority to bind and loose, to connect and to let go.[38]

Living in the light, the church is also called to go to hell:[39] to be in the company of those cast out onto the edges of existence, in the company of those who totter on and over these edges. This is to say, the church is called to descend to the dead. Why else would Jesus have said to Peter, "the gates of Hades will not prevail against it" (Matt. 16:18), when he spoke of the church? And where else will the God of reversals be able to meet us and raise us to new life?

Binding and loosing. Connecting and letting go. As we respect this rhythm, we the people who are the church, who are Christ's risen body, attest to our faith, fearful not of death but of death in life that does not lead to life abundant. For "the glory of God is human beings fully alive,"[40] as Irenaeus of Lyon affirmed in the second century. And I add, in the words of Paul to the Corinthian Christians, it is our calling to "do everything for the glory of God" (I Cor. 10:13, NRSV).

Two

A Heart for Hospitality

For to dare to hope to *become*—to dare to trust
the changing light—is to surrender the dream
of safety.[1]

*I*was on vacation in northern New Mexico when I felt a
sore spot on my right breast in the shower one morning.
A wave of anxiety went through me and out of me. I instantly
rehearsed reasons why this sore spot could not possibly indi-
cate breast cancer. First of all, in my innocence, I thought I
was too young. I was, after all, only thirty-five at the time.
Then again, if it were cancer there would be a distinct lump
not a vaguely defined sore spot, I argued. Finally, I breathed,
it must be some sort of something related to my menstrual
cycle. My rehearsal thus concluded, I resumed my vacation.

Or I tried to do so. In retrospect, I have to confess that not
too far from my consciousness was crystalline clarity: I had
breast cancer. In my marrow, blood, and bones, I knew. Nonetheless, not until a friend's urging sounded urgent did I sched-
ule a mammogram a week after returning to Chicago.

I went for my mammogram on Monday, August 6, 1990.
Hiroshima Day. Forty-five years later another bomb exploded.
My world was in rubble . . . again. Everything I had thought
was important was instantly trivial. These things fell away.
My life was invaded, then altogether occupied by doctors, by
consultations and tests, by the hospital and the cancer center.

The results of the mammogram were alarming. But, of course, a diagnosis could not be determined without a biopsy. My biopsy, which was on Thursday, August 9, Nagasaki Day, became a lumpectomy. While I was still in the recovery room, I knew what I knew with even more certainty. I saw the striken face of my surgeon. And, as I later read with recognition in Audre Lorde's *Cancer Journals*,[2] I was *cold*, chilled to the bone. Even with an enormous pile of blankets. My body knew.

The news was not news, then. Instead I felt as if when the word "cancer" was spoken to me a brand was burned into my body. Branded: MORTAL. DYING. I felt this despite the fact that the lump in my breast was so small it had not been palpable on physical examination, despite the fact that, therefore, initial prognostic indications were promising. Nonetheless, I felt as if I no longer belonged in the land of the living. I had descended to the domain of the dying, the soon to be dead. And, whether I die in a few years from a recurrence of cancer or at age ninety of feistiness, I will live in the borderlands between the living and the dead. Consciousness of death crystallized in this way does not dissolve.

Startled by the swiftness of my descent to the dead, I was also amazed at the atmosphere of the cancer center, an atmosphere I have found to be the same here in Rochester as in Chicago. Specifically, I was not prepared for the silence pervading the waiting rooms. No one spoke to anyone. Gradually, I have guessed that these rooms are silent since to speak to another cancer patient is to confirm one's own identity, an identity silence seems to cloak. I have also wondered whether the silence was anticipatory, since, as Audre Lorde wrote, death is "the final silence."[3]

I confess I did nothing to break the silence. I did nothing to connect with the other cancer patients in my company. In part, my own silence spoke of my ongoing incredulity about what was happening to me. I walked in and out of waiting rooms and offices more outside than inside my body. In part, however, my own silence in these spaces testified to my terror, lest speech unleash a torrent of grief, the grief of which J. M. Coetzee writes in his novel, *Age of Iron:* "grief past weeping."[4] The passage, whose words are spoken by the central character, a woman with breast cancer, continues: "I am hollow. I am a shell. To each of us fate sends the right disease. Mine a disease that eats me out from the inside."[5] Thus, from the beginning of my experience with breast cancer, I was, most of all, overwhelmed with loss.

The loss that held me in thrall did not have a literal referent—the loss of my breast—as for so many women diagnosed with breast cancer. Even then, I knew my sense of loss to be much more amorphous, much more ancient. It has taken me the subsequent four years to name the overwhelming loss I felt. It is the loss of love in my life.

As I wrote in the introduction, love has not been lost in my life because I have not been loved. I have been blessed by parents, by a sister and brothers, by hosts of friends, and by lovers, teachers, and colleagues, with wondrous love. But it has taken me many years to *know* I have been and am so loved. Too long I have been blinded by a sense that I was not lovable, even more precisely by a sense that I was not worthy of love.

My sense that I was not lovable was attached to all the ways I did not "fit" society's fashion of lovability. I have said in the introduction that I was nearly six feet tall already as an early adolescent. At the same time I also had acute acne and wore braces to "correct" my buck teeth. My periods started when I was nine years old. By then I was also wearing a bra. I wanted to hide, crawl under a bed as I indeed did one afternoon while changing clothes to water-ski with a friend.

Born into a radical reformation religious tradition, this sense of bearing no signs of lovability was compounded by a sense I was unworthy of love. I was suckled on shame and on "holy hatred of the self."[6] I was schooled on self-sacrifice.[7] I sang, "*if* with his love he befriend thee,"[8] with reference to God's love. The message concentrated in this hymnic phrase was the pervasive message with which I grew up: one was loved if one was worthy to be loved, and one was worthy only when one loved one's neighbor selflessly.

This worthiness is not the worthiness of which Audre Lorde wrote, and which I cited in the introduction: "Know we are worthy of touch before we can reach out for each other." The worthiness of which Lorde wrote is born of learning to love one's self, born of a sense that one is lovable, a sense on which one's ability to love and accept love is predicated. The worthiness with which I grew up was born of the moralistic mandate to love others self-sacrificially, paying no attention to one's self, based on the assumption that somehow one was thereby saved from one's unworthiness. I remember my mother remarked, time after time, that according to the Gospel injunction, love of neighbor was predicated on love of self. I even repeated her point! But deeper still was my sense that love of self was selfish.

Breast cancer catalyzed a crisis of nurturance: my own. I was nudged toward suckling and being schooled on love of my self. More precisely, my blind eyes were opened as people—mostly women—poured love lavishly on me at the time of my diagnosis and my surgeries, and on through the weeks I underwent radiation and the months of my recovery of endurance and energy. I saw signs of love all around: flowers on my doorstep when I returned home from a radiation treatment; casseroles in my refrigerator; my lawn mowed; cards and calls from friends in Chicago, friends back in Cambridge and Virginia, and friends across the country and around the world; dinner invitations; offers of rides to radiation or to doctors' appointments, etc., etc. I remember, with a certain amount of chagrin, I remarked to a friend at one point: "I don't know what to do with all this love!"

In time, I was able to call on this wondrous love to be present to me in the place I felt most abandoned and alone. During the weeks of radiation therapy, lying atop the cold steel table, my arm over my head to expose my tattooed breast to the rads, I wrote and intoned this poem, "Liturgy for Life":

They said, "Just like two small beauty spots";
I heard, "permanent tattoos"
and numbers on Auschwitz arms
bombarded my brimming eyes.
My woman's life-bearing body
has been marked and machines scream
day after day
souvenirs of Civil Defense sirens
conjuring the perjury of protection,
"duck and cover,"
while my breast is naked to the waist.
Stubborn like limestone soil
I celebrate my own daily office
laid out like a burnt offering
on their unholy table
I convert this to be my sanctuary
whence I call forth the cloud of women
who will heal me:
pray for me now in the hour of my need.
And I am anointed.

My breasts are becoming wilder.
I am filling up feisty, sweet with sweat,
tough as teak, tender as tendrils
to petal plentifully.

In more time, I learned there was only one thing I needed to do with all the love: let my self be loved. For me, however, this one thing needful was the hardest thing of all. It was hard because it meant healing the wound of unworthiness in me. It was hard because it meant seeing my self as lovable. Letting my self be loved meant graciously gathering all the hidden and hated parts and pieces of my self, loving them, and loving my self. But, if this one thing needful was hard for me, it had already been hard for others. A friend from graduate school made this point poignantly when she recently said to me: "It was hard for those of us who wanted to love you."

Slowly, slowly, it became harder and harder for me *not* to find my self worthy, lovable. Toward the end of my six-week radiation therapy, I wrote a poem, "I Glow In the Dark," that testifies to this coming change of heart:

> it is harder and harder to hear
> —days revolving like doors—
> him tell me to raise my arm
> to bare my red-faced breast.
>
> were former days
> held fast by unholy necessity,
> making my own flesh
> the price I'd pay?
>
> I can bear it no longer.
> my hunger for my own heart
> comes home ranting and raving
> rifling this reticent routine.
>
> I'm shrieking shamelessly,
> haggling this time 'round
> for all I'm worth.

As if this discovery were not enough, there was an attendant, a devastating discovery: I am not really able to love others *unless* I love myself! This discovery was devastating, although not new. After all, it is the Great Commandment as I had heard it from my mother and had, in turn, intoned myself. The discovery was now devastating because it meant that the very thing on which my worthiness to be loved depended— love of neighbor—was made impossible by my inability to love my self. Love does not discriminate in this sense. If I withhold love from my self I withhold love from others. I withhold love because my heart is hardened, not by malice, but by moralistic highmindedness hewn from hatred of my self.

I began to learn these lessons about love as my blind eyes were opened by people who persistently presented signs of love I could no longer pass over, without falling over. I also learned lessons about love when I met Mrs. Curran at the time I was receiving radiation therapy. Coetzee's *Age of Iron,* which was published that October, is written in the form of Mrs. Curran's letters to her daughter, who has shaken the dust of South African apartheid from her feet and moved to America.

The novel begins the day Mrs. Curran, a retired classics professor living in Capetown, drives home having heard from her doctor that her breast cancer is carving into her bone and that she will die. Mrs. Curran, like her daughter, has abhorred apartheid. But, until these latter days of her life, she has been shielded from the flesh and blood of its horror, and from the rage it has incubated. Eventually, her home is literally invaded by the reality of the rage and horror, by the malignancy killing her country as surely as cancer is killing her.

A homeless man, Vercueil, shows up in the alley down the side of her garage, smelling of "urine, sweet wine, moldy clothing, and something else too. Unclean."[9] This unsavory man, slowly but surely, becomes Mrs. Curran's companion. Eventually, she invites him into her house and, in time, even into her bed, where they lie "folded one upon the other like a page folded in two, like two wings folded: old mates, bunkmates, conjoined, conjugal."[10] On the eve of her death, Mrs. Curran's perspective on how Vercueil has come to be her companion has changed. She writes to her daughter:

> I have fallen and he has caught me. It is not he who fell under my care when he arrived, I now understand, nor I who fell under his: we fell under each other, and have tumbled and risen since then in the flights and swoops of that mutual election.[11]

The one who imagined herself to be the inviter, the hostess, now sees she has also been invited, is also a guest in her own house.

When I first met Mrs. Curran, altogether predictably, I was most fascinated by her struggle to love the unlovable. One night, another stranger—John, the surly friend of her domestic's dead son Bheki—shows up at Mrs. Curran's house seeking a haven from the police. She writes her daughter:

> So this house that was once my home and yours becomes a house of refuge, a house of transit.
>
> My dearest child, I am in a fog of error. The hour is late and I do not know how to save myself. . . . Slowly, reluctantly, however, let me say the first word. I do not love this child. . . . I love you but I do not love him. . . . This is my first word, my first confession. I do not want to die in the state I am in, in a state of ugliness. I want to be saved. How shall I be saved? By doing what I do not want to do. That is the first step: that I know. I must love, first of all, the unlovable. I must love, for instance, this child. Not bright little Bheki, but this one. He is here for a reason. He is part of my salvation. I must love him. But I do not love him. Nor do I want to love him enough to love him despite myself. . . . I cannot find it in my heart to love, to want to love, to want to want to love.
>
> I am dying because in my heart I do not want to live. I am dying because I want to die.[12]

I say my fascination with Mrs. Curran's struggle to love the unlovable was predictable because these remarks resonate with the spirit of my earliest formation in terms of self-giving, selfless love. These remarks resonate with my earliest reckoning of the Gospel call to love the outcast—the tax collector, the prostitute, the halt, the blind, and the lame—not only those who are clean or those with whom I am comfortable. I have reckoned the Gospel call is to love not only the like-minded or my own kind, but the Other this terrorist-crazed culture teaches me is a threat to my way of life.

Now rereading Mrs. Curran's story, I am most fascinated by the fact that this crusty character let herself *be* loved by one so unlovable as Vercueil. I am fascinated by the fact that, at the end, she sees she needs his solicitude, however fumbling. I am fascinated, and frankly frightened, as I see her once hardened heart changed into a heart for hospitality: hospitality over which she does not finally preside as hostess. It is the still unsavory stranger, Vercueil, who holds her when she dies.

My changed perspective on a heart for hospitality—and, accordingly, my rereading of Mrs. Curran's story—has been profoundly influenced as I recently reread the Gospels together with the Bible study group with which I meet weekly here in Rochester's 19th Ward, my neighborhood. I have seen with new eyes: Jesus was not the host, he was the guest when he sat at table with the tax collectors, prostitutes, and sinners of his time!

My previous reading of the Gospel stories was informed by the paradigmatic image of Jesus as the host at the Last Supper, the prototype of the Eucharist. I had been taught, and I had thought, Jesus was and is the one who invites all—including the halt, the blind, and the lame as well as tax collectors, prostitutes, and sinners—to the table to keep the feast. Suddenly I saw and I see that Jesus *accepted* the invitation of those considered to be unsavory characters. As Jesus did so, he let himself be loved by those who had become strangers relative to the religious communities of his day.

These insights about love—about loving and accepting love—are shaping my work as an ecumenical leader and theologian. These are times of tremendous change, often attended by turmoil, in the ecumenical movement as well as in the churches.[13] Some lament languishing commitment to organic church union—the vision of one church, united in governance and structure as well as in matters of doctrine, ministry, and liturgical practice, a union that would involve the death of many forms of church heretofore known—and speak about stagnation.[14] Some say Christianity's inculturation into Asian, African, Latin, Caribbean, and Pacific cultures is not syncretistic,[15] as is often charged, but is similar to Christianity's earlier inculturation into Greco-Roman and various Western cultures. Some say the diversity that thrives on this inculturation will deepen divisions, not nurture unity. Some say we can no longer speak of unity at all, inasmuch as this notion is irredeemably laden with Eurocentric images and intimations of monolithic power. Some say the search for the unity of the church is based in the unity of the biblical witness. Some say the biblical witness, and the life of early Christian communities, was as disparate and diverse as are the churches today.[16] Some say the problem is "reception," this is to say, the churches' lack of regard for what has already been achieved ecumenically, particularly in the last three decades. In contrast, some say ecumenical leaders have misunderstood "reception" as a deluge of documents pouring from the top down rather than as attention to the ecumenical life thriving at local levels. The change to which these and other voices testify becomes tumultuous insofar as these points of view become charges and countercharges rather than calls for conversation.[17]

Running through what have most often been charges and countercharges is the claim that the most serious issue facing the ecumenical movement is discerning acceptable limits of diversity.[18] This claim emerged most fiercely in the aftermath of Professor Chung Hyun Kyung's presentation to the Seventh Assembly of the World Council of Churches in Canberra, in 1991, only months after my breast cancer diagnosis and treatment. Professor Chung began her presentation with an invocation of "the spirit of Hagar, the Egyptian, the black slave woman exploited and abandoned by Abraham and Sarah, the ancestors of our faith," "the spirit of Jephthah's daughter, the victim of her father's faith, offered as a burnt offering to God because he had won the war," "the spirit of Joan of Arc, and of the many other women burnt at the 'witch trials' throughout the medieval era," "the spirit of earth, air, and water, raped, tortured and exploited by human greed for money," "the spirit of soldiers, civilians and sea creatures now dying in the bloody war in the Gulf," "the spirit of the Liberator, our brother Jesus, tortured and killed on the cross," among others.[19] She then spoke of her homeland Korea as a land of "spirits full of *Han*," this is to say, spirits full of anger, resentment, bitterness, grief.[20]

In response, many members of the Orthodox Church and many evangelicals—with whom many longtime European and American ecumenical leaders stood in silent solidarity—said, for example:

> We must guard against a tendency to substitute a "private" spirit, the spirit of the world or other spirits for the Holy Spirit who proceeds from the Father and rests in the Son. Our tradition is rich in respect for local and national cultures, but we find it impossible to invoke the spirits of "earth, air, water and sea creatures."[21]

Chung replied, saying that the talk of syncretism masked the more profound question raised by her presentation: the question of power. She continued, with reference to Western, male theologians who have heretofore set the limits:

> We have been listening to your intellectualism for 2,000 years . . . please listen to us. . . . Third-world theologies are the new paradigm, the new wine that can't be put in your wineskins. . . . Yes, we are dangerous, but it is through such danger that the Holy Spirit can renew the church.[22]

Danger, indeed. Chung herself has been harassed by threats of death and more since her presentation in Canberra.

Not surprisingly, for it follows from what I have written above, I do not believe the brokenness between and among the churches—a brokenness that calls the credibility of the churches' witness in the world into question[23]—will be healed if we define the most serious issue facing the ecumenical movement in terms of the limits of acceptable diversity. This is not a new thought for me. I have long argued, in articles and in speeches, that talk about the limits of acceptable diversity invokes images of exclusion not embrace.[24] In these articles and speeches, I have often referred to the story of Abraham being a host to the strangers who appeared at the door of his tent on the plains of Mamre[25] and, accordingly, to the verse in the Letter to the Hebrews about thereby entertaining angels unawares.[26] I have only recently reckoned that talk about the limits of acceptable diversity implies our identity as hostesses and hosts who do the inviting, but who do not deign to accept an invitation from a stranger, surely not from an unsavory stranger.

I agree with Professor Chung, what is at stake here *is* a question of power, more particularly the loss of power on the part of those who previously have held position and privilege. Indeed, I hear ecumenical leaders who have called for inclusivity nonetheless cling to the power to decide *who* the "other" voices will be, and how inclusive is inclusive, as well as the power to determine when and where trespass occurs. The power of binding and loosing, in other words, is still held in the hands of these few and not all the faithful.

Accordingly, I believe the challenge before the ecumenical movement is not how to draw the limits of diversity, is not how to identify who is acceptable and to whom we will offer hospitality on the basis of whom we agree with. The challenge is to wrestle anew with what we mean by "unity." I agree with Letty Russell, who remarks: "The ecumenical watchword of 'unity' needs every bit as much critique and discussion of limits as does diversity."[27]

Russell's remark follows her reflections on hospitality. I am indebted to Russell's reflections inasmuch as she suggests a way through and beyond the difficult discussion of unity and diversity may be to speak instead of hospitality and diversity.[28] She says: "Hospitality is an expression of unity without uniformity, because unity in Christ has as its purpose the sharing of God's hospitality with the stranger, the one who is 'other.'"[29] Most helpful to my own reflections is her reference to the work of John Koenig, who writes in *New Testament Hospitality:*

> *philoxenia*, the term for hospitality used in the New Testament, refers literally not to a love of strangers per se but to a delight in the whole guest-host relationship, in the mysterious reversals and gains for all parties which may take place. For believers, this delight is fueled by the expectation that God or Christ or the Holy Spirit will play a role in every hospitable transaction (Heb. 13:2, Rom. 1:11–12).[30]

But I believe to speak of reversals is not to speak plainly enough to the point. I believe the heart of the challenge is to relinquish[31] the position and privilege that allows powerholders to presume to be the inviters, the hosts or hostesses, in the first place. The challenge is whether the churches who are members of the ecumenical movement will let themselves *be* chosen, *be* invited as guests, *be* loved by those we have been taught threaten "Christian identity" or complicate, perhaps undercut, possibilities for church unity. I believe those who have had the power are called, in the words of Professor Chung, to lay down talk of limits, and then to listen long enough to be able to hear the strange voices speaking to us. Only thereby will we be able to accept invitations to sit at table with strangers who may, by God's grace, become mutual partners.

Two examples of the apparent inability of the ecumenical movement to be, in this sense, mutual come to mind. First, I was involved in the restructure of the National Council of the Churches of Christ, U.S.A., during the late 1980s. This task was initiated in 1987 when the Committee of Fifteen was appointed to prepare a report proposing a new structure, including revised bylaws. At the same meeting, a committee was appointed and charged with cultivating relationships between the Council and Pentecostals, Evangelicals, and Roman Catholics. Not altogether aware precisely why I was so profoundly disturbed with this plan at the time, I have later come to understand. The National Council was, on its own terms and in its own time, preparing the table, as it were, to which the "others," the strangers, would then be invited.

Another equally disturbing example is the ordination of women. The movement to ordain women to the ministry of word and sacrament, most particularly among churches of the Protestant reformations, coincides with the contemporary ecumenical movement of the churches toward visible unity. These movements have been mutually influential, not least because the visible unity of the church has been understood to involve recognition of those called and ordained as ministers as well as recognition of the baptism of members. But, by the beginning of the twentieth century what has continued to be clear was already clear: if the question of the ordination of women were brought to the forefront of discussion, the goal of church unity would recede. Anglican bishop and ecumenical leader William Temple is often quoted in this regard. In 1916, he said: "I would like to see women ordained; . . . desirable as it would be in itself, the effect might be (probably would be) to put back the reunion of Christendom—and re-union is important."[32]

The apostolic letter, *Ordinatio Sacerdotalis*, issued by Pope John Paul II on May 30, 1994, deepened concern about conflict over the ordination of women in the ecumenical movement. The letter was and is a matter of concern particularly because it seems to foreclose further discussion. The Pope is clear in this regard: "I declare that the church has no authority whatso-

ever to confer priestly ordination on women and that this judgment is to be definitively held by all the church's faithful."[33]
This unilateral declaration threatens not only the movement
toward church unity. Catholics themselves, already divided in
this debate, are more deeply divided than ever.

Indeed, the depth of intra-Catholic conflict makes it clear
that the inability of the ecumenical movement to accept invitations to be guests at tables presided over by others—whether
women or other strangers!—mirrors the inability of the
churches themselves to be gracious guests. It is hard to imagine
churches' change of heart, hard to imagine a heart for hospitality generous enough to accept invitations and to sit at table
with the likes of Pentecostals or Evangelicals or Holiness and
Wesleyan and Reformed sorts or the United Fellowship of
Metropolitan Community Churches or charismatics or faithful
members of religious communities other than Christian.

Here, I am helped by Julia Kristeva's *Strangers to Ourselves.*[34] In this book, Kristeva addresses one of the most burning, indeed incendiary, issues of our time: the influx—even
encroachment in the eyes of many—of strangers. In societies
around the world, so-called foreign workers or exiles or refu-
gees or illegal aliens are appearing. Kristeva addresses this new
situation by exploring the history of foreigners in Europe, a
history not unrelated to the history of foreigners in America.
For my thinking about hospitality, Kristeva is most helpful
when this exploration leads her to her main point: we will
never be able to live well with the strangers appearing around
us unless we are able to live well with the strangeness—the
otherness—in ourselves.

So I return to my earlier remark about graciously gathering
all the hidden and hated parts and pieces of myself, loving
them, loving me. I see that accepting the hospitality of
strangers, being with others, is first and foremost about accepting my self and being with my self. I agree with Audre
Lorde, who wrote in a second book of essays on her cancer

experience: "I have always known I learn my most lasting lessons about difference by closely attending the ways in which the differences inside me lie down together."[35] I would add, or by closely attending the ways in which the differences inside me do *not* lie down together. In short, the problem I—and the churches in the ecumenical movement—would project out there belongs within ourselves. Unless addressed, it will—like cancer—kill us from the inside out.

My ecumenical theology, therefore, is as trinitarian as my ecclesiology. The trinity is at once a communion of persons *ad invicem*—"turned to face each other"[36]—that is, an open communion, "integrating and inclusive."[37] "Its end," says Leonardo Boff, "is the full glorification of all creation in the triune God, healing what is sick, freeing what is captive, forgiving what offends divine communion."[38] Only what Boff refers to as an "a-trinitarian monotheism of the churches"[39] can support the unity and diversity debate, with attendant and distorting debates about acceptable and unacceptable, about identity and syncretism, etc.[40] A trinitarian perspective on ecumenism sees that it is only as we are with others—most of all as guests of those we think are unsavory strangers—that our own identities are clarified. It is a vision of mutuality, radical and risky—even dangerous—inasmuch as it will threaten what we have known.

Here I am heartened by the recent statement of the Groupe des Dombes, *For the Conversion of the Churches*.[41] The Groupe des Dombes writes:

> Christian identity is always a Christian becoming. It is an opening up to an eschatological beyond which ceaselessly draws it forward and prevents it from shutting itself up in itself. Thus it is a radical opening up to others beyond all the walls of separation.[42]

In this sense, says the Groupe des Dombe, "the Spirit has priority over the church, which obliges the church to acknowledge the Spirit's initiative and thus not to set its own bounds."[43]

Only, through the power of the Spirit—which "blows where it chooses" and "where it comes from or where it goes" we do not know (John 3:8, NRSV)—as we dare to lay down talk of limits, dare to be loved and well as loving, and so dare to accept invitations, will the churches' common life in Christ become the body of God's Risen One, who so often sat as a guest at table, most frequently with unsavory and strange sorts.

Three

The Promise of Presence

It is hopelessness even more than pain
that crushes the soul.[1]

I wanted to curl up in a corner and die. But my limbs were leaden. My thoughts were too tangled and tenuous to focus on accomplishing a feat so strenuous. So I sat—a zombie—slipping out of my body into isolated space, unaware of time's passage or people talking. I myself was stripped of speech.

Just days before my June 1993 descent to death's door my embrace of life had been energetic, enthusiastic. Indeed, the entire spring I had been in a state of elation. I experienced a rare creative release, an avalanche of activity and articulation. My mind cavorted—feisty and frisky—as I attended to the myriad tasks associated with preparations for the inauguration of the Program in the Study of Women and Gender in Church and Society at the Divinity School here in Rochester, as well as with teaching. My body burst with perpetual productivity. Sleep seemed superfluous. So did eating. Typically shy in social settings, I was now confident, sometimes scintillating.

In short, and in retrospect, I see the exuberance so characteristic of my childhood, and at times since, was exaggerated. To try to calm my self that spring, I turned to alcohol on occasion. This made sleep more possible at times. Then, in the second week of June, I plummeted, plunged precariously. Sleep was more than ever a stranger. My body's desires—activity, ardor, appetite—were deadened. I sat amid shards. My world was in rubble . . . yet again.

This was not the first time the icy fingers of depression had held me in thrall. Countless times throughout high school, college, and graduate school my high energy exuberance had crashed into inertia. I became depressed or my body manifested my distress as another illness, or both. Then and there my everlastingly evasive sense of self-esteem dissolved into a never-too-distant sense of self-hatred. Everything I endeavored to do seemed wanting, worthless. Moreover, I wondered and worried when the failings and faults of my abilities and accomplishments would be found out. Accordingly, my childhood abandonment anxiety awakened, for I assumed that when my failure *was* found out everyone and everything would be taken from me; I would be bereft and altogether alone.

As if anticipating or even already enacting this abandonment, I engaged in self-destructive acts, particularly in graduate school as my depressions began to become more frequent and frightening. I drank. I smoked, I cut my self. I did not cut my self with the conscious intention of hurting my self. Nonetheless, altogether alienated from my body and paying no attention—my head out on holiday—I cut off tips of fingers, cut deeply into fingers, when wielding kitchen knives, etc. Moreover, I indulged fantasies of my demise at my own hand.

Most frequently, especially in my senior year of high school, these fantasies were fantasies of hanging. As editor of the school yearbook that year, I had a key to a small room on the second floor. Here I sequestered myself, hour after hour a truant thanks to the small bathroom built into the already small room! Here I poured out poetry, poetry that pronounced my fascination, frankly friendliness, with death by hanging:

> go away world
> leave me not
> trembling in your heart strings!
> Draw the shade

> tighten the string
> close into night
> the fearful day.
> leave me not
> to writhe and pour
> over small but tremulous
> dailies.
> Race with the shade
> pull with all reserve
> close in, release
> leave me not so!

Years later I wrote a poetic retrospective of this time:

> Noose-necked
> I'd stand
> staring down demons of dread,
> sure my soul's secret
> was sturdy solitude.
> Perched above the parking lot:
> hideaway
> hellhole.
> Even as I enunciated
> my perilous pain
> I was impervious
> to the slit in my soul's lining,
> leaking
> into my gut, my grip
> ferociously fastening
> 'round realms of rage
> great gales of grief.
> How shall I have
> my heart's habitation?
> With what sew the tatters
> of my silken soul?

For years I thought these tortuous sensibilities were signs of some moral failure or fault on my part. A veritable walking, talking Pelagian! A latter-day Anabaptist indeed. If I were worthy of happiness and love in life I would *be* happy and loved. Surely I was doing something wrong, something that made me deserving of these descents to the doors of death. My sense that such was my lot in life was deepened as I noted that depression was once termed "melancholia," a word derived from the Greek word for blackness, "melos." Melanie is also derived from "melos." My nemesis was my namesake, I reckoned, and I felt fated as I regarded my failings and my faults.

Although I now know mood, and, for me, attendant energy, swings from high to low and back again—often with increasing frequency and severity unless properly treated—are connected to aberrant biochemistry amid the neurotransmitters of the brain, I was not altogether off the mark in wondering what I was doing "wrong." I say this because more and more analyses, historical and contemporary, make it clearer and clearer that many more women than men have been diagnosed as depressive, or insane or mad or mentally ill. Jeffrey L. Geller and Maxine Harris, in *Women of the Asylum: Voices from Behind the Walls, 1840–1945,* write in their introduction:

> Each age defines "acceptable" or "ideal" womanhood in a particular way, and women who do not conform to those standards often find themselves ostracized or punished in some way. Regrettably "treatment" in asylums for the insane was one way of dispensing with some women who did not fit the mold of acceptability. . . . The mere possession of a female body was thought to increase one's vulnerability to madness, and women who could not or would not adapt to their life circumstances were especially at risk.[2]

Stephanie Golden puts the power differential determining these judgments in sharper relief:

> Historically women have been subject to different "expectancies" and had less power than men. Defin-

ing specific women as insane had to do not only with
what was "wrong" with them but with the social
norms that dictated how women ought to behave, in a
context where someone else had the power to enforce
those norms.[3]

I have long known that my body has not mirrored the norm
of womanhood in Western societies. Indeed, in this regard, my
body has been a bloody battleground, as well as a Foucaultian
site of social control. This is to say, although I surrendered
much of my carefree childhood spirit, my body continued to
resist such circumspection: a resistance manifested in myriad
aches and ailments.

I was, nonetheless, not ladylike: decidedly not. When I was
a child, my mother admirably attempted to anticipate my being
a lady. She clothed me in beautiful dresses complete with crino-
lines and lace collars. I myself preferred being shirtless with
my brothers. And as I grew, being smart, strong, strong-
willed, tall, etc.—all these things that meant I did not "fit" the
image of ladylike—were in my eyes evidence of my moral
failure. My failure to "fit" was my fault. I did not yet see this
as a feature of a sociocultural setting, of an ethos, that had
exiled the nonrational, made "madness" a matter of guilt, and
introduced "treatment" intended to re-enroll women into com-
pliance with moral values centered in the patriarchal family.[4]

The clinical character of my depression—and its self-
destructive bent—was first detected following my long hospitalization and near-death experience in 1982. When I walked
out of the hospital I did so on the condition that I would be
in psychiatric care. Although I dutifully, albeit resentfully,
made an appointment and saw a psychiatrist, I did not fill the
prescription for the antidepressants I was given. My resentment about all this was the face of my fear. I *had* been found
out! My not filling the prescription was a protest. More profoundly, it was my attempt to live on in the isolated secrecy I

had thought would protect me from the fires of judgment: unworthy!

But during the summer of 1982 I descended into an even deeper depression. So severe I was scared. I then had to tell my psychiatrist of my ploy and get another prescription, which I filled forthwith. I continued to take antidepressants—the old generation of antidepressants called tricyclics that gave me cotton mouth—for seven years, although I ended psychotherapy after two years, when I moved from Cambridge to Chicago.

My next major depression was in early December, 1989. A year later, in December 1990, as the Gulf War was about to erupt, I remembered that time of war within and wrote these two poems.

> *"(Ad)Vent"*
> flesh and blood burn off   what breaks
> voices on the radio military-logic mad
> is night   no relief for human fodder
> insomniacal vigils instituted
>
>
> war ignites within   consolations of a lifetime
> crack   customs rattle like seedpods
> I voice raids on my wireless   will no one
> tune in   serenity shrieking   to my wave
>
>
> lightbulbs burst on lighting   I sit in shadows
> stagger in space   pock-marked   cobwebbed
> faded cloths   flapping   patch basement panes
> touching nothing   nothing touching
>
>
> full body alarm   four a.m. awake again retching
> bloodied rags   flung in my face   shuddering
> to be alive at all   after all   I become
> the cry   no comfort comfort not   in this wilderness

"You Asked"
What do I think
my self under siege
up against the urge
to preserve to protect
in my fell clutch of circumstance

Nothing there to think
I am not   you see
separate or solid   only a shadow
about to stray out of time
on roads I cannot reveal   lured   I

crack   thin-threaded cracks   leak
through cracks   cannot contain my life
my grief   my glory   cut flowers
suckled on still born water
sunrays can't revive   such polite polluted skies

What do I think
only the cessation of concept or continuity
on peripheries of perception   so why
this cerebral prowling   I await an Armageddon
my body politic beats at the walls   wailing

Sleep was scarce. I awakened at four A.M. morning after morning. Pounds burned off my body in minutes, it seemed.

My psychotherapist, whose work with me brought the relief for which I was desperate, was suspicious of antidepressants: "Who told you you're depressive? You're living a depressing life! Let's work on it!" My sensibilities about my depression being my moral failure surged full force. I immediately quit taking antidepressants: cold turkey. Not until June 1993, in the depths of my most severe depression to date, did I once again resume antidepressant therapy.

I had returned to psychotherapy already in February 1993 to address issues arising after I left a nine-year relationship in the fall of 1992. More particularly, I got back into therapy because getting involved in a brief rebound relationship brought me face to face, once again, with betrayal: this time my betrayal of my self. I saw I was betraying my self because, once again, I was searching for a sense of worth from someone or something outside my self. So doing, I had abandoned my self, activated against my self my age-old anxiety about *being* abandoned.

After my superlative spring, the severity of my depression— a descent far beneath more familiar "blues" or doldrums— signaled to my therapist a major affective disorder: manic depression or bipolar II, since my severe depression alternates with a mild hypomania, not fullblown mania. The psychiatrist to whom she referred me confirmed the diagnosis for me in August, 1993, and prescribed an anticonvulsant, carbamazepine, as well as an antidepressant, zoloft.

My response to the diagnosis, to hearing the word "bipolar" spoken to me, unleashed a torrent of grief and rage and relief. I was grief-stricken because, again, I felt branded: MAD. MENTALLY ILL. The whole weight of our society's judgment landed on my head, justifying my sense of guilty unworthiness. I wanted to run, to take cover, to tell no one, lest I be exiled as so many have been, whether on ships of fools or in attics or asylums. I was enraged because this torment by which I had been held in thrall had not been named and properly treated until my thirty-ninth year. Had no one noticed?! Had no one *wondered?!!* Why had my refrain, time and time again, been a plea unanswered: I need relief! I need relief!

At last I was relieved. I am relieved. This relentless rhythm is not ignominious recompense for my failures or faults. The demon dragging me to death's door has been named and thereby domesticated. The demon is not dead. I will always and forever be watchful—yes, also from time to time worried—regarding signs of recurrent swings. But I believe those icy fingers can not take me captive as before.

Amid all the grieving, the raging, and the relief, this diagnosis—this naming—has been a purifying fire, as I put it in the introduction. The burden of my sense of moral culpability has burned away, along with the acidity of society's judgment. Purified of this terrible twofold sentence and attendant punishment, I am present to my self, and therefore to others, as never before.

When I speak of presence I speak, first and foremost, of presence in my body. I live, and think, in my body, no longer alienated or abstracted as I have been most of my life. I delight in my body's desires—sensory and sexual. I savor the pleasure of aromas and beauty, of taste and touch. I honor what my body knows. More particularly, I live, and think, in my female body. I have come out as a woman! I come out convinced that what matters, for men as well as women, in the face of society's stultifying code of conformity is for each one to affirm our own uniqueness and our finitude, so we are able to respect and risk being changed by the reality of otherness.

When I speak of presence I also speak doxologically. This is to say, I speak of the glory *(doxa)* of God's presence: "Why are you cast down, O my soul, and why are you disquieted within me? Hope in God; for I shall again praise . . . my help and my God" (Psalms 42:11, NRSV). Nowhere is this presence more profoundly pronounced for me, especially given my experience of manic depression, than in Psalm 139:

> Where can I go from your spirit? Or where can I flee from your presence? If I ascend to heaven, you are there; if I make my bed in Sheol, you are there. If I take the wings of the morning and settle at the farthest limits of the sea, even there your hand shall lead me, and your right hand shall hold me fast. If I say, "Surely the darkness shall cover me, and the light around me become night," even the darkness is not

dark to you; the night is as bright as the day, for darkness is as light to you (Psalms 139:7–12, NRSV).

Put profoundly to the point, presence heals hopelessness, heals hopelessness that resigns and reckons reality is fated and so sets up barriers against our selves, one another, and God. To speak of presence, then, is also to speak of communion. To speak of presence is to speak of communion that is already among us as we live amid the overflowing life of God's triune communion. To speak of presence is to speak of communion that is anticipated in hope wherever the struggle for survival and life abundant still goes on. The promise of presence is, in this sense, what Paul Ricoeur has spoken about as an "affirmation . . . [of] the restoration of [human] positivity,"[5] as an "upsurging of the possible,"[6] on the other side of ennui, exile, and evil.

I remember reflecting on presence, perhaps for the first time, when I read Brita Gill's essay, "A Ministry of Presence,"[7] as a graduate student in the early 1980s. At that time, amid all the talk about responsible action that attended the constructive theological task, I was impressed by Gill's insight into "the minister's manner of being with another."[8] She was clear and convincing: "It is a ministry of being, not merely of doing:"

> I cannot heal another person; I can only create the environment and relationship where God's healing may take place. . . . My first act of engagement with another person should be one not of self-assertion, but of making a space where the other feels his or her presence is received.[9]

For Gill, therefore, presence to our selves and one another is the way of being that prepares us to receive God's revelation, revelation that is not knowledge of God's nature so much as it is "the unfolding of an ever-faithful Presence."[10]

When I recently reread Gill's essay, I began to see that this presence to our selves and one another and God—this revelatory presence—is a way of being that prepares us to be persons of authority. As is already apparent from my reflections on what it means to be the church in chapter 1., I have long been convinced that genuine authority is not the authority invested by place or position. Rereading Gill, I see what I sensed: authority derives from presence.

Ralph Harper makes this point when he writes: "All presence has authority . . . One whose presence makes others come alive is one who is alive and real. . . . Presence can be explosive, liberating, revealing, quieting. Presence has force and authority."[11] A ministry of presence is, thus, a ministry of being "alive and real" and making "others come alive." It is *thereby* a ministry invested with authority.

I have been helped in my exploration of these emerging connections among presence and ministry and authority by Kathleen B. Jones's essay, "On Authority: Or, Why Women Are Not Entitled to Speak."[12] Jones argues that, given the typical analysis and understanding of authority in modern Western political theory—an analysis and understanding that has wide cultural currency as "a set of rules governing . . . action" or "a set of practices designed to institutionalize social hierarchies"[13]—women qua women are separated from the sphere of authorizing.[14] Jones specifies her argument by saying that the commonly accepted "dichotomy between compassion and authority contributes to the association of the authoritative with a male voice."[15]

Having advanced her argument, Jones goes farther than the feminist critique that accounts for this association by analyzing the separation of public and private spheres, and their attendant ascription as male and female spheres. Jones says, "the feminist critique of authority as a specific form of male privilege has not focused enough on the limitations of traditional concepts of authority. . . . I would suggest that authority currently is conceptualized so that female voices are excluded from it."[16] Following Foucault, Jones continues, "the dominant discourse on authority silences those forms of expression linked . . . to 'female' speech" and "secures authority by opposing it to emotive connectedness or compassion."[17] Echoes of the Enlightenment exile of unreason and madness!

Jones then deconstructs the prevailing understanding of authority, of what she calls a disciplinary, controlling, rule-ordered concept of authority. In its stead, she articulates an understanding of authority as a "contextual, relational process of communication and connection"[18] or, in other words, "a way of cohering and sustaining connectedness."[19] Reminding us of what Hannah Arendt has already noted,[20] namely that the Latin root of the word "authority" is "to augment," Jones also articulates "authority" as "the construction of a meaningful world" and as an addition of "meaning to human action by connecting that action to a realm of value and to justifications for action beyond criteria of efficiency and feasibility."[21] This sense of authority does not, as the dominant notion does, "abstract human will and agency from the meaning of living as mortals in a world filled with those who are different from us."[22] Rather, it is "out of this emotive connectedness to others that genuine authority as the augmentation of the texture of daily life emerges."[23] This understanding of authority is profoundly akin to Harper's understanding of the authority of presence: being alive in a way that makes others alive.

Jones's notion of authority is also akin to the notion articulated by Letty Russell in *Household of Freedom: Authority in Feminist Theology.*[24] Letty Russell writes about "partnership as authority *in* community" and "partnership as an authority of freedom that uses people's need for solidarity and care to empower them through a relationship of mutuality."[25] Accordingly, she calls on us to live these new images, thereby subverting the patriarchy forms of authority as domination, of authority dictated by a divinely ordered hierarchy from top to bottom: God and man and woman and children and other living creatures and plants and so-called material nature. In contrast, Russell tells us "the major clue to finding our way into a new metaphor for relationships of authority in community" is to pay attention to what is now viewed and valued as the bottom: to the poor and marginalized—I would add mad—challengers to white, middle-class, educated, pious points of view.[26]

Jones's and Russell's reimagining of authority raises a point of tension I think is characteristic of the post-Enlightenment West. On the one hand, we continue to live with the rhetoric of the traditional paradigm of authority being established by corporately acknowledged past precedent—"age-old rules, values, and powers"[27]—and exercised externally on the basis of office or order. This appears from time to time as authoritarianism. On the other hand, we live with the legacy of the nineteenth-century romantic paradigm that privileged the authority of individuals as imaginative authors, i.e., authority as internal authority.[28] Accordingly, from time to time, this appears as anarchy.

Carter Heyward clarifies the way in which these tensive paradigms coexist among us:

> . . . a doctrine of internal authority has free rein among us today—provided that we locate and accept our own interests as compatible with those of white, ostensibly heterosexual, affluent christian males. Upon others—marginalized people, sexual deviants, and political dissidents, for example—external authority characteristically is brought to bear in forms of force and punishment.[29]

We are at the end of the era in which either option on the terms of this paradigm is life-giving. Still, as my asides about authoritarianism and anarchy suggest, and as Hannah Arendt reminds us:

> The end of a tradition does not necessarily mean that traditional concepts have lost their power. . . . On

the contrary, it sometimes seems that this power of well-worn notions and categories becomes more tyrannical as the tradition loses its living force and as the memory of its beginning recedes.[30]

With this, I recall a remark made by German novelist Christa Wolf, a remark that again associates life-giving authority and presence. She says: "How one could be there and not be there at the same time, [is] the ghastly secret of human beings in this century."[31] Having been severely depressed and experienced exaggerated energy, my body knows what it is to be there and not be there at the same time. This makes Wolf's remark not only clear-sighted but bone-chilling to me. My body knows self-destructiveness pervades this experience, whether personally or corporately wrought.

In this age of absent presence, and especially amid my own experience of this alienation, I hear the Gospel anew on the matter of authority. As I read and read the Gospel narratives again, I begin to believe authority is bearing witness in one's body—word and deed—to the Good News so people can see and come to seek promised life abundant. Authority cannot accomplish this by command or control. For bearing witness is revelatory, not regulatory. Authority as bearing witness is revealed in persons who themselves in their lives incarnate the proclamation that Christ is risen, that God's new creation in Christ is already present. And authority as bearing witness is revealed in persons whose life together—as *ekklesia* or as *oikoumene*—makes manifest God's unfailingly faithful presence among those whom prevailing values judge unlikely or unlovely. Authority as bearing witness is, in short, self-authentication—whether of a personal or corporate self—derived from revelatory presence that is mutually life-giving.

Speaking of self-authentication, I am reminded of a phrase in an essay by Mercy Amba Oduyoye. She refers to her grandmothers as women who "carried their own heads" and says: "Carrying your own head is not the same as naming yourself (the latter is autonomous). It is a concept that implies listening to the community and letting your self-determination be shaped by a vision of its ideals."[32] "But," Mercy makes clear, "I cannot be alive in a community that ignores my existence."[33] The authority that derives from revelatory presence is not possible unless the uniqueness—including the wisdom—of each person and of the other is mutually recognized and respected.

Those of us who are relatively possessed of—or by—power and privilege need to practice letting go in order to participate in the revelatory presence from which genuine authority derives. The witness we bear in our bodies will be credible only as we repent and relinquish pride of place among all people. It is too easy for any and all of us to vie for eternal victimhood. It is too easy for any and all of us to be eternal victims.[34] In either instance we abrogate the self-responsibility attendant to self-authentication. The responsibility of which I speak is not driven by regulations or rules. The responsibility attendant to authentication, and therefore to authority, is participation in the task for which we were created in God's image. This is the task of *poesis*, mutually making and remaking who we are and are becoming, making and remaking the world in which we live, confident that creation is not completed. Participating in this task, I believe we come to know and make known in our bodies our selves the promise of presence as revelatory. This is the authority with which we can together reforge foundations for our future.

I have been heartened in this belief—in the belief that the authority derived from revelatory presence is "the restoration of [human] positivity," is "an upsurging of the possible"—as I read the story of the 1929 "Women's War" in Nigeria, a story told in the novel *I Saw the Sky Catch Fire*.[35] The women went to war because the men themselves did not start a war when the colonial government—the White man—counted the men and imposed a tax. To make matters worse, to pay the tax the men pawned not only farm implements; they pawned their

wives' beads and broke the taboo against selling pregnant ani-
mals to raise money to pay their taxes.

The Women's War began in the third or fourth year of this
taxation. Things were bad, very bad. Inflation was wildly increasing. Crops were failing. Then the colonial government
proposed to count the women for the purpose of taxing them
as well. The White man assumed that because the men had
been counted without much conflict there would be even less
conflict as a consequence of counting the women.

But the war began. It began because the women were united
in a way the men were not. The women were united, not
because they had leaders: "in truth Ndom had no leaders."[36]
The women were united by what their bodies knew of grief
and rage:

> Every woman was led by her own intimate knowl-
> edge of their common grief and sense of injustice, by
> what Nne-nne called Woman's Grief. One by one and
> all together, they seemed to have known about this
> grief from the time they were little girl infants suckling
> milk from their mothers' breasts. They knew about it
> from the lullabies their older sisters sang in order to
> quiet them and rock them to sleep on hot, lonely after-
> noons when their mothers were at the farms:
>
> Little sister, little sister, please stop crying
> Lest I throw some sand in your eyes!
> Remember the time Grandmother went to prison in
>   the sky
> And set the sky on fire!
>
> Ndom set the sky on fire! Drew down lightning from
> the sky and set the earth on fire!
>
> Daughters learned of Woman's Grief from their
> mothers. Married women confirmed it for one an-
> other as they toiled. . . . They knew of it in them-

selves and they recognized it in one another. *A woman knows what every woman knows!*[39]

Of course, a chorus of charges accompanied the outbreak of the Women's War: "Insane! Irrational! Mass hysteria, like the spirit-induced madness that possesses some of them during some of the juju festivals! A sudden overflow of premenstrual or postpartum hormones! Spontaneous combustion!"[38]

The women persisted: waged war. And when the White man came to count them—"How many are you?"—the women chorused: "Ndom is one, uncountable upon uncountable, but still one. Undivided."[39] The White man—who "made and broke laws as he went along, shook hands to treaties he had no intention of keeping, violated oaths the same day, week, month that he swore them[40]—was altogether bewildered. No one was in charge, but their sense of belonging to one another was palpable.

Thereby the women waged war. Not with "guns or strong talk, but with . . . the awesomeness of the Solidarity of All Womanhood,"[41] a solidarity, a communion, that

> joined the rich woman to the poor, the prostitute to the virgin, the young girl who had just had her first monthly period to the old widow who could no longer remember when she had had her last. Women in prisons. Women on the farms and in the markets. Women on their way to the well. Women on their way to the bushes to find firewood. The aura of Womanhood rose from the earth and descended from the sky and covered everything in a convulsive swirl. . . . Even the madwoman . . . was heaved by its power.[42]

The women—a crowd of two thousand—marched to the District Office of the colonial government. They chanted. They wielded sticks and kitchen knives and pounding pestles, waving them in the faces of the District Officer and his soldiers. Then, "as if on cue,"[43] the women turned together to face away from the White man. The women "doubled over, turned up their buttocks and aimed them at the approaching White man. Then they pulled up their loincloths, so as to expose their naked bottoms."[44] Faced with this "field of female bottoms, fat and lean, old and young, brown and black, and at every stage of the monthly cycle,"[45] the soldiers shut their eyes. "They felt like throwing away their weapons and running."[46]

"An upsurging of the possible" indeed! The Ndom knew and made known in their bodies the promise of presence, presence that is revelatory and thus reforges foundations for a life-giving future. Even amid a chorus of charges: Insane! Irrational! Mass hysteria! Madness! The women were coming home, coming home from exile to set the earth on fire! A purifying fire! Burning off the bondage of outside officers, authorizing one another by being women together.

We, men and women, are thereby ministers to one another. We are ministers to one another as we create places of presence, places wherein we make known the promise of revelatory presence. We are ministers to one another as we thereby create places wherein God's healing may happen.

Four

Telling the Truth

I tell myself that life is the long struggle to
understand and love fully. That to keep faith
with those who have literally saved my life and
made it possible for me to imagine more than
survival, I have to try constantly to understand
more, love more fully, go more naked in order
to make others as safe as I myself want to be. I
want to live past my own death, as my mother
does, in what I have made possible for others
. . . the people I believe in absolutely, men and
women whom death does not stop, who honor
the truth of each other's stories.[1]

Knowing what my body had long known—I am a lesbian—I had to conjure the courage to choose life, not
death. This was the heart of the deep depression that hovered
all around as familiar faces and figures fell away in front of me
and I floated headfirst into a tunnel that opened behind me in
the spring of 1982. And the "roaring inside"[2]—an announcement that I was not ready to let life go—was a roar of rage
and grief: How had I internalized the myths and norms of
this society's heterosexual setup, even though I thought I had
resisted more than most? How had I internalized these myths
and norms so thoroughly that death seemed my only choice if
I could not, would not live accordingly? The "roaring inside"
was my mighty and momentous "NO!" to this death in life for

me—to death itself—and my "YES" to being alive as I believe God has created me to be. A woman who loves women. A lesbian. The "roaring inside" was coming out to myself.

I had initial inklings of my sexual identity when I was in college. During these years my closest connections were with women. In some cases these connections were passionate, although not, strictly speaking, sexual. My connection with one woman was particularly passionate. But when we came into conflict fraught with heat and fire, affect for which friendship did not seem to account, I was nonetheless stunned—indeed, shamed—by my mother's question: Are you homosexually involved?! No! I quickly, and altogether unthinkingly, answered. And that was that.

Perhaps amid the aftershocks of my mother's question, perhaps out of a more diffuse and desperate desire to be "normal"—both are retrospective reckonings—when I went to Harvard Divinity School the following fall I did my damnedest to *be* "normal." That summer I went shopping with my mother and bought clothes for my wardrobe that had devolved into frayed jeans and faded T-shirts in college. And in September, when a bright and handsome history graduate student wanted to date me, I said "Yes."

Indeed, at Christmastime during my second year at Harvard, I said "Yes" to his proposal of marriage. My mother was as shocked by this announcement as she was by my announcement, four years earlier, that I felt called to ordained ministry! My father was characteristically quiet, but clearly concerned. Their responses were, in some measure, reflections of their own lives. My mother was twenty-nine years old and my father was thirty when they married after seven years of courtship. But my father's response was also marked by his sense that I was not radiant, not really happy. And—as he later blurted out—his response was even more profoundly marked by his sense that I was settling for marriage to a man who, in his words, was "not strong enough" for me.

I broke my engagement the following September. Not primarily because of my parents' responses. In the meantime, more inklings of what my body knew about my desires had made their way into crevices of my consciousness. That summer, the summer of 1978, walking down Massachusetts Avenue, from Central Square toward Harvard Square, I was suddenly flooded with sadness. Sadness rolled over me in waves, then sucked me into an undertow, as I realized that, if I married, my relationships with women would become in some measure secondary. My relationship with a man would be assumed to be primary. I would be expected to make a life—a daily life—with a man. I did not and do not dislike men qua men. But, suffused by sadness, my body knew then and knows now that my connections with women are my most passionate and most meaningful. I was heartbroken. I still feel my face, a mask, stiffened as I stared straight ahead and walked unblinking onward.

The cracks in my consciousness were more powerfully widened by my connection with one woman in particular. We had met four years earlier—my mother had introduced us—and had stayed in touch since then. Her mind was scintillating. Her laughter was lyrical. And she saw *me*, recognized me as me, not as an extension of herself or as the incarnation of some ideal. Just after our engagement, my fiancé and I visited her, her husband, and their two sons. We met again in the summer of 1978. She was by now separated from her husband; the attraction I had always had to her specified the more amorphous sense I had had on the Cambridge street.

But these scenes were still sketchy. My awareness of all this at the time was but barely nascent. I broke my engagement in September 1978 and spent the third year of my M.Div. study seeing one or another of two men who were more attracted to me than I was to them. Then, in September 1979, having decided not to pursue doctoral study without taking a break and having dramatically burned all the application forms I had amassed, I arrived in Geneva, Switzerland, to study for six months or so at the Ecumenical Institute, cosponsored by the World Council of Churches and the University of Geneva.

There I met the first woman I knew—body, mind, and spirit—I wanted to touch, to whom I wanted to make love. I did not know these feelings when we first met. My attraction—intense and passionate—to her was familiar, and in this sense safe. But then I was offered an internship with the Faith and Order Secretariat of the World Council of Churches that would keep me in Geneva another six months—until the first of September 1980—and she decided to stay with me rather than return to Berlin. Then, in August, I had thoughts of staying with her—in Geneva, where I had been offered a three-year position with Faith and Order, or in Berlin, where I would find something . . .—and awareness tore torrentlike through the cracks in my consciousness.

When I left her in Luxembourg, whither we had traveled together for my Icelandic Air departure to Dulles, it was my heart that was rent. An awful cleavage. But one I still considered anomalous in my life. To stanch the flood of fear as well as sadness I saw a man during the first few months I was back in Cambridge beginning my doctoral study. Until the cracks in my consciousness widened, and I pitched to and fro between waves of awareness. "Lay you out in lavender!" a friend quipped. Lay me out, indeed! Mortified, I wanted to die.

A few weeks after this annunciation, my back went out as I bent over to dress in the locker room of the YWCA where I regularly swam. I had been horsing around—God forbid, flirting?!—with a woman with whom I had had a brief affair a few months before. I felt as if a bullet blasted into my back. Recovering enough to hobble around the corner to the apartment that was then home, I called my psychiatrist to cancel my appointment later that day. My psychiatrist returned my call: "I don't care *how* you get here: Get here! You can't continue to beat up your body and be self-destructive because you love women."

This was six months before I nearly did die over it all. It was a year and a half before I made love with the woman who had the scintillating mind and the lyrical laughter, the woman with whom I was in a relationship until the fall of 1992. The woman with whom I was in a relationship until a voice I my self did not know cried out: "Please don't ask me to give my own best self away again!" And I knew that the self I had become in order to survive had turned against my own best self. I my self had abandoned my self out of my longing for love, for being loved. And then there was the toll taken by the silence that surrounded and suffused all the years of this relationship. Of course, close friends knew, and my family. But being an ordained minister, being employed by a church institution and active ecumenically, the message was clear and unequivocal: Be silent. So I was.

Now I know what my body has long known and made manifest in myriad aches and ailments. What I know is well wrought by Audre Lorde's oft-cited phrase: "Your silence will not protect you."[3] Homophobia—by now venomous and vindictive—has taken on the spirit of medieval, and sixteenth- and seventeenth-century witch-hunts.[4] Simply being single— not married to a man—is reason enough to be suspected. Living with a woman is a dead giveaway, unlike ten or twenty years ago when women could live together without charges being brought. More than this, there is, as Virginia Mollenkott has put it, a "price" to be paid for "passing" as someone other than who I am created by God to be.[5]

The price to be paid for passing takes various forms. There are the feelings of being left out, of being invisible, in various social settings. There is the torture of trying to make a relationship or a living arrangement acceptable, presentable, so to speak. There is the stress that accrues . . . and also alienates.

But, for me, all these and more taken together do not add up to the highest price of passing, the price I can and will no longer pay. This highest, indeed death-dealing, price for me is perpetrating a sin of omission. Silence *is* a sin of omission. It is a sin of omission not only because silence is dishonesty to others, and to my self. What is even more unlivable for me is this: by being silent, by perpetrating the sin of omission, I omit my self from being the fullness of the image of God as God created me to be. I thereby put God's glory at risk as well as my own being, for, as Elizabeth A. Johnson makes clear, God's glory is dimmed whenever and wherever women and men created in God's image are diminished or violated. God's glory, says Johnson, is women, and men, fully alive.[6] I am fully alive—no death in life—as a woman loving women, as a lesbian.

So I still believe the truth sets free! The truth sets me free to be who I am created by God to be. And I believe I am created by God to give glory to God for and as who I am. Put in other words, I am created, not to explain or to justify, but to enjoy and to be joyous being a lesbian, being a lover of women. I am created to celebrate, as I did when I wrote this poem, "Blasted with Ecstasy":

> Waiting is by word of mouth
> mouth   round   open   reckoning
> Now she is here
> and we are face to face
> So I know waiting is not resolved
> in silence by speaking alone
> As I knew when I touched her tasted her
> fire in fingers   tongues torchlike
> licking life into her entrances
> she into mine   flourishing
> As I knew when we came into each other
> when shouts split sheer
> her cleft and mine   chins full tilt
> blasted with ecstasy   We know
> it is from the flowering of flesh
> heaven's wild honey wine flows
> flows over   over flows   over

> earth's mounds and mouths   our
> breath between us
> windblown   blowing us out
> over earth speaking her blessing
> on our hunger honored.

After writing this poem I rested from relationship. I spent nearly a year being present to, with, and for my self.

I now know in this space of presence I was making my self ready—this time really ready—to choose to be with the woman for whom I wrote the following poem. In this poem I delight in love I know now as I have not known it before, love become a dwelling place—body, mind, and spirit—with this woman, my partner:

> moments are made holy
> by laughter's blessing
> in the belly of love
> flesh and blood
> shout the sacrality
> of well-met
>
> So let us keep the feast
> ecstasy splashing
> in and out
> of cups we cradle
> at one another's lips
>
> our ode to joy
> draughts of heaven
> come down to earth
>
> whereupon our feet
> fly free as wind
> and face to face
> we kiss
> now and now's eternity
> dancing our desire.

Seeing me dwelling in love with this woman—seeing me radiant in the fullness of my being—I see my father's face beam a blessing.

My concern, therefore, is not to rehearse the issues of Christianity and homosexuality per se.[7] Although I am all too aware that these issues are among the, if not *the*, most church-dividing issues of our day, my concern is whether we can recognize and respect one another as uniquely created in God's image well enough to engage in conversation—well enough to honor the truth of one another's stories—in hope that the Holy Spirit, the Spirit of love as well as truth,[8] may move among us. I believe we will thereby be set free to be together the people of God, our life together an icon reflecting and revealing the intricate integrity of God's life of communion.

I know from my life and death wrestling with being a lesbian, with telling the truth about being a lesbian, that to tell the truth is to participate in God's revelation, which, as Chung Hyun Kyung says, is located in our life itself.[9] To tell the truth—lay my body bare—is to realize the promise of revelatory presence of which I wrote in chapter 3.

To tell the truth about my life, about who I am, is to participate in the realization of God's revelation, since as Christians we confess that the truth is not propositional but personal. Jesus Christ, we confess, *is* "the way, and the truth, and the life" (John 14:6, NRSV). And when Pilate asks, "What is truth?" (John 18:38), Parker Palmer points out that the falsity of Pilate's perspective is indicated by his word "what."[10] Jesus is not a teacher of truth—objective and out there—but is truth.

To say truth is personal is not to say that it is privately so, that it is simply subjective. We Christians also confess Christ to be the Risen One, whose *body* we are. We know truth when we are in conversation as members of the gathered body, which is the risen body. Parker Palmer writes:

> [Christ's] call to truth is a call to community—with him, with each other, with creation and its Creator.

If what we know is abstract, impersonal, apart from us, it cannot be truth, for truth involves a vulnerable, faithful, and risk-filled interpenetration of the knower and the known. Jesus calls Pilate out from behind his objectivism into a living relationship of truth. Pilate, taking refuge behind the impersonal objectivist "what," is unable to respond.[11]

This call to truth telling is a call to community that is answered in conversation. A community of conversation is a community of the Risen One in which members give account of the hope that is within them. A community of conversation is a community of the Risen One in which members honestly and honorably hear one another's stories of their lives.

Truth telling calls for a community in conversation for another reason. If we lay our bodies bare in our world so inhospitable to truth and to vulnerability we need to be in the company of others—a communion of saints, indeed—who choose to live with thin skins.

But the call to truth telling as a community in conversation calls us beyond any and all exchanges of words. We are called to become the flesh of our words. I still shiver, shudder, as I write this thought. I shiver, shudder as I write this chapter! The climate of our times is so inhospitable to truth. Our cultural media craft words to confuse and cover and control. The attack on truth tangled in an attack on language. Technique—rent from flesh and blood reality—is taken to be truth. Deception is affirmed as a survival strategy![12]

No wonder the climate of our times is even more inhospitable to vulnerability. Sometimes our resistance to vulnerability is right-headed, since it is searingly in touch with the epidemic of violence virtually everywhere. Sometimes our resistance to vulnerability is the face of our fear. Still shivering, shuddering, I stand with Dorothy Allison who says:

> I wear my skin only as thin as I have to, armor myself only as much as seems absolutely necessary. I

try to live naked in the world, unashamed even under attack, unafraid even though I know how much there is to fear.[13]

I stand, convinced that precisely here and now—when neutrality and numbness are taken to be true humanity, and when violence threatens our very humanity—I choose to befriend my fear. So doing, I choose to lay my body bare, to tell the truth of my body as battlefield, the truth of my body created to glorify God. I still believe truth sets free, even from the bondage born of violation and the threat thereof. I choose to lay my body bare here and now because hope is threadbare and because I am convinced with James Baldwin: "Revealing one's nakedness . . . is, really, our only human hope."[14]

I first began to think of truth telling as baring my body, becoming the flesh of my words, when I met Mrs. Curran during the fall I underwent radiation therapy. We met Mrs. Curran in chapter 2 as I wrote of what she taught me about loving and being loved. Here I take us to the scene of Bheki's death. Bheki is the son of Florence, Mrs. Curran's domestic. The scene is set on a rainy, stormy night. Bheki has disappeared. Mrs. Curran is out in the storm searching for him, together with Florence and Florence's schoolteacher friend. They witness the burning of a black township before they finally find Bheki. His bullet-ridden body is laid out in a rain-punctured school hall.

Mrs. Curran is suddenly set apart from the people with whom she has come to this place. She is also aghast at the suffering suffusing the scene. This suffering is, for her, a symbol of the suffering of time immemorial. She shivers, wet and weary as well as alone. But Mrs. Curran does not duck for cover. Possessed by a courage whose prophetic clarity is crafted out of pathos, she walks up to a nearby group of soldiers. Afterward, writing to her daughter, she asks:

> What did I want? What did the old lady want?
> What she wanted was to bare something to them,

whatever there was that might be bared at this time, in this place. What she wanted, before they got rid of her, was to bring out a scar, a hurt, to force it upon them, to make them see it with their own eyes: a scar, any scar, the scar of all this suffering, but in the end my scar, since our own scars are the only scars we can carry with us. I even brought a hand up to the buttons of my dress. But my fingers were blue, frozen.[15]

Truth, Mrs. Curran confirms for me as she bears witness with her body, is not a possession. We do well to be wary of whatever persons or groups claim as truth. For to tell the truth is *to be* possessed, as Mrs. Curran was possessed, by a message that comes to us to upset the safety and security we would preserve and protect.

We who would be possessed prepare ourselves by being present to ourselves, to one another, and to God—by recognizing the promise of revelatory presence—as I have affirmed in the previous chapter. The promise of revelatory presence is realized when we also lay our bodies bare, ready and willing to become the flesh of our words.

I speak of laying my body bare, not of *being* laid bare, not of violation. I speak of a choice, a choice made after counting the cost of doing so in our violent society. There are many ways in which I may choose to lay my body bare, choose to become the flesh of my words. I do so as I write this chapter. I do so as I write this book on what my body knows.

Thinking of our time so inhospitable to truth and even more inhospitable to vulnerability, and of truth telling as the choice to become the flesh of my words, I think also of the practice of preaching. I make the connection between truth telling and preaching for at least two reasons. First, I think of preaching because the pulpit is one of the few public places wherein, by God's grace, we may become the flesh of our words. I also relate my thoughts about truth telling to preaching because so often the pulpit is the last place wherein the freedom of the Spirit of truth and love blows beyond the declamation of a dead and deadening letter.

Preaching, this is to say, is not first and foremost the proclamation of the Word. Preaching is an announcement. The distinction I make is this. Preaching is not simply the proclamation of the Word that has already come into the world—Word become flesh—for the Word is the Word of the living God who still reveals God's self in the world and in our lives. Too much theology is written and too many sermons are delivered as if God were dead, as if God were not revealing God's self afresh and anew each and every day. Preaching is, in this sense, not the proclamation of a dead and deadening letter. It is an announcement of the Good News that is *news* addressed to us today.

The Good News—the Gospel—comes to people who, in the imagination of Walker Percy, are "castaways" on an island we assume to be home. We pretend to be home on the island where we have washed ashore amid the waves. And our ships—the institutions we have heretofore taken to be church and family and the church united, and so on—are no longer seaworthy. Percy puts it plainly:

> To be a castaway is to be in a grave predicament and this is not a happy state of affairs. But it is very much happier than being a castaway and pretending one is not. This is despair. The worst of all despairs is to imagine one is at home when one is really homeless.
>
> But what is it to be a castaway? To be a castaway is to search for news from across the seas. Does this mean that one throws over science, throws over art, pays no attention to island news, forgets to eat and sleep and love—does nothing in fact but comb the beach in search of the bottle with the news from across the seas? No, but it means that such a message will come, and that one knows that the message will

not be a piece of knowledge or a piece of island news
but news from across the seas.[16]

Preaching the Good News is an announcement that comes, as
Paul Ricoeur—with a Barthian accent—puts it, "from the
other side."[17] It is an announcement that is unanticipated. As
unanticipated—and unlikely—an annunciation. An announcement that shatters and shakes up our perceptions and perspectives. Moreover, acknowledging all we know about the creative
power of words, I believe, as we preach the Good News that is
news, we may become flesh of our words, may make manifest a
new way of being in the world. Then and there God may
choose to reveal God's self as the living and ever-creating One
in our midst.

So preaching is not simply an act of announcement any more
than it is proclamation. Preaching may, by God's grace, be an
act of realizing revelatory presence. Hannah Arendt speaks
about revelatory presence in these words:

> The revelatory quality of speech and action comes to
> the fore where people are with others and neither for
> nor against them—that is, in sheer human to-
> getherness. Although nobody knows whom he [or
> she] reveals when [she or] he discloses himself in deed
> or word, he [or she] must be willing to risk the
> disclosure.[18]

For Arendt, the doer of deeds—however good—who does not
disclose self, will not participate in the promise of revelatory
presence realized. H. Richard Niebuhr, in his classic, *The
Meaning of Revelation,* confirmed the primacy of self-
disclosure when he said of God's revelation: "what is revealed
is not so much the mode of divine behavior as the divine self."[19]

I think it is significant that Arendt highlights this experience
of presence by portraying it in a spatial rather than in a tempo-
ral frame. This is to say, I think it is significant that she chooses

to say "where," rather than "when," "people are with others."
Arendt thereby stakes out a claim on the spaciousness of revelatory presence. She stakes out the space of presence wherein
we may choose to lay our bodies bare, wherein we may choose
to tell the truth of our lives.

Novelist Kate Braverman captures and conveys the significance of the space of presence in the following passage from
her novel, *Palm Latitudes:*

> Space [is] fertile as the sandy loam alongside deltas,
> a womb. The void [is] not empty but merely waiting.
> What men call space [is] simply the belly between
> barren cycles and abundance. All women know this,
> thinning and going fat, condensing the possibilities,
> weaving the fabric of all things, committing the ulti-
> mate sorcery and letting it flow between their legs
> like rain or waves. Oceans were born this way,
> snakes, and comets, rituals and science, lava, infants
> and stars.[20]

Women's bodies, Braverman says with specificity, know that
possibilities for new life may spring amid the space of presence.

Attending to what our bodies know, we may yet tell the
truth of our lives. We may yet reclaim our birthright: be who
we were and are created by God to be. Gertie, the uprooted
but resilient woman in Harriette Arnow's *The Dollmaker,* got
it right referring to our birthright: "I guess . . . we all sell our
own—but allus it's easier to say somebody stole it."[21] Too easy
for any and all of us to vie for eternal victimhood. Too easy
for any and all of us to be eternal victims, indeed.

But Gertie, uprooted but resilient—not mistaking the island
for her home—believed. She who believed awaited a message
from another shore, knowing all knowledge is revelation. A
womb leaping. Annunciation. Announcement. Good News of
"who" more than "what." Appearance of self out of entangled
estrangement. Full appearance. Being fully alive. "The shining

brightness we once called glory,"[22] which is still possible if we dare to speak our selves: tell our stories, testify to our spirits, lay our bodies bare. Shining brightness still possible as we thus bear witness in the public places.

And as Naomi Goldenberg has said:

> As women speak more and are heard more in public settings . . . Hermeneutics might then discover the original text, that is, the human body. In the beginning was definitely not the Word. . . . It is flesh that makes the words.[23]

Words no longer empty or evasive. No longer become flesh as brutal or destructive deeds. But words bearing witness to our selves born of flesh in the image of God, whose Spirit is the Spirit of life and love, and of the truth that sets free.

Poetic Interlude
Standing

a word   I waited on a word
this word for this day
to come and craft a meaning
a message from me to you
on this threshold   throbbing
We stand—awaiting
acclaimed—together in hope

I waited and I was visited
—all knowledge is revelation—
so I still believe
angels watch and keep us
demons possess
and I still believe
the shining brightness once called glory
is possible   palpable
since we inhabit a spirited space
a visitation you see
late at night at last
at long last daybreak
chronos cracked

I know this moves toward madness
transgression
of appropriate ascription
word and deed
it is
the breaking down

or is it up
of yes-saying to what is
male ruled   female reconciled
the breaking through
as co-creators
of what will be

daybreakingnight   nightbreakingday
words moved through me
Maya Angelou conjured herself to me
I rummaged for her words
at the dawning of this nation's hope
then stumbled into memory   my own
stirred up her images as they inhabit me
trees rooted sturdily
exiles excruciatingly grafted
morning greeted graciously
and I wept
raging wind rattling windows
the spilling over of forbidden feeling
free at last   at long last free

so I know
our memory does not fail us
unless we determine to dwell therein
dig in   fall back
on a sea of stars   on peace all night
or an epidemic of threat
parts of our selves parceled out
pieces of life   broken off   litter left
lingering over loss   banishing blessing

This morning I stand on meeting
a miracle   gifted   glory made manifest
I wonder
are we able to imagine truth

I stand on meeting
old sadness made new enchantment
I wonder
are we able to imagine hope

This morning I stand on meeting
and   yes   on greeting
since I believe there are places
—I know where nightmare nestles
the tremulous ache of betrayal's avalanche
the ferocity with which grief gnaws
the petulance of fear's patina
infernos ignited by plundered pasts
the beauty of who we are
making it hard to be who we are—
and I still believe there are places
to take root   freely flourish
gather all the parts and pieces
homemaking hallowed   bringing honor
day by day deliberate
places to ring doxology
rhythms drumbeat regular
lest drumstruck despair distill
or disappear down deep
taking hostage our delight

I stand on meeting
we will walk into a new country
our own procession   yes Virginia Woolf
daughters and sons
women and men
authored selves   self authorized
our own truth spoken
our love lived out
death's walled-in streets done in

our own procession
into life abundant

I stand on meeting
and I still believe
in visitations
angels unawares attendant
as we walk step by step wayward
they do not fear to tread

daybreakingnight   nightbreakingday
Good morning   our life flows on
the meaning ours to make
I stand on meeting
and   yes   on greeting

Five

◈

God's Glory and Neighbors' Good

Perhaps the world will end in fire and the Lord will come—it is not for us to say. But it is for us to say . . . whether hope and faith will come back into the world.[1]

I write what I write the way I write to have a say in bringing hope and faith back into the world. I write to keep hope alive and to heal the fracture of faith on earth. And I write to wrest a blessing from the faithful Presence I name God, to be healed by the Risen One who I believe bodies forth hope for abundant life.

It is not at all incidental that the text of my first Hebrew Bible exegetical essay as a theological student was Genesis 32:22–32, the story of Jacob wrestling at the Jabbok. I have, as the preceding pages attest, wrestled and I have not let go. I have wrestled, and people and places have bestowed a blessing. I believe angels watch and keep us.

And I am still wrestling. Not least because the times in which we live are threshold times. I stand on Holy Saturday, straddling tensive days of drama. We live amid signs of hope and signs of danger, signs of faith and signs of despair: all jumbled and juxtaposed. I believe living in these times we are "living in the interregnum," to borrow a turn of phrase by Nadine Gordimer, who in turn echoes Antonio Gramsci.[2] I believe, this is to say, we are living between the times and the orders of things. We are privileged to witness and to participate in a passing away and a coming to be. There is never one without the other. We can, of course, choose to keep company with those preoccupied with survival and shoring up sagging structures. We can also choose the ways we can greet the future that *is* coming, with or without us.

Nadine Gordimer, in an essay entitled "Living in the Interregnum," addressed this choice with courageous clarity. She said, with reference to her home country, South Africa, which has since she wrote stepped across the threshold:

> In this interregnum, I and all my countrymen and women are living. Ten thousand miles from home, I speak to you out of it. I am going, quite frequently, to let events personally experienced as I was thinking towards or writing this paper interrupt theoretical flow, because this interaction—this essential disruption, this breaking in upon the existential coherence we call concept—is the very state of being I must attempt to convey.[3]

Gordimer's choice constituted her "claim on the future," which she is convinced rests on "how to offer *one's self.*"[4]

As I have written herein I too have chosen an "essential disruption." It is a disruption I believe to be a holy disruption. Its holiness is altogether as ambiguous as Rudolf Ott reckoned.[5] Neither fascination nor terror has been far from me as I have undertaken this disruptive task.

I still wrestle. Amid the debris of former theological formulations. So it is time to take up the task about which I wrote in the introduction. Having told the stories of my life—laid my body created to glorify God bare—it is time to discern and distinguish contingency from the features of a new course to be charted. I do so as I thread these features together with my theological meanderings to this moment.

I think I have always been a theologian. I have, as long as I can recall, been asking why we are at all? and for what we are created? I have been relentlessly wrestling to name the One whose Presence has forever been faithfully palpable: "Where can I go from your spirit? Or where can I flee from your presence?" (Psalms 139:7, NRSV). But I have not often been inclined to accept answers I have been offered.

This theological spirit within me is inscribed in a poem I wrote when I was in high school, "A Metaphysical Primer":

> i saw them go that evening
> South it was, and it made me believe
> those days weren't really over
> only waiting to return.
> the world is round they tell me.
> do doubters then go tumbling
> over edges?
> or fly on the wings of southward geese
> to where?
> ah, i, earthen creature that i am
> dream.

My thinking in those early days was as an earthen creature. My body and mind and spirit were intimately rooted in the earth of the Shenandoah Valley of Virginia. Thinking my thoughts, I especially loved to be ensconced in the deep darkness atop Maymont Farm. Held in the night, hallowed to my inhaling nostrils, I wrote "Lunar Reflections":

> have you ever flirted with a whippoorwill
> as dusk is moving over the fresh-plowed earth
> and a mind is laboring with rubble
> newly-planted?
> the clear call sails forth on night's sweet air
> i join nature
> wink to the moon
> and answer.

My theological musings were also nurtured, as I accompanied my mother when she preached, and then as I preached, up and down the Shenandoah Valley and all through the surrounding hills and hollows.

These early years of my theological formation were characterized by a sense of community. Growing up in the Church of the Brethren was like growing up in an extended family. For better and for worse. I grew up knowing that I belonged to a people of God. I grew up believing this particular people of God bore witness in its life together to the convictions and values confessed: to nonresistant pacifism; simplicity of lifestyle; service to sisters and brothers of whatever creed or culture around the world. The community's self-understanding as "sect"[6] was thereby woven together with ecumenical engagement.[7]

Indeed, my formation in the Church of the Brethren first taught me about relinquishment, about letting go for the sake of life abundant. Early in my life I learned of various service projects to which the Church of the Brethren had given formative leadership—Heifer Project, Agricultural Missions, International Christian Youth Exchange, CROP, etc.—and I learned my people had let them go so that as ecumenical projects they could have a life fuller than any one church could sustain. In short, it was in the Church of the Brethren that I learned my earliest lessons about connecting and letting go, about binding and loosing.

I learned these lessons in a painful way as well. And so I must confess—as I have earlier intimated—that my experience of community has more often manifested the view I eschewed than not. This is to say, my experience of community has often manifested Parker Palmer's characterization of communities as being created by acts of exclusion.[8] At the end of my college years I attempted to escape from what I felt to be the cost of being in, not out: the cost of conformity, theologically as well as personally. And having returned to work on the national staff of the Church of the Brethren after my doctoral study, I felt and feel the price to be paid for belonging is even higher. My people have become more and more acculturated to the culture. I say this as I see concern for church growth, evangelism, and sexual ethics overrides earlier equal emphasis on economic, social, and political issues of justice and peace. And as the nonconformity to the culture that attended conformity within the community is thereby attenuated, I sense—not altogether unpredictably—a more and more alienating separatist spirit within the Church of the Brethren.[9]

I sense this spirit inasmuch as the Church of the Brethren has yielded to the timeless temptation to set up as idols certain perceptions and conclusions created in our own end-of-the-twentieth-century image. The Church of the Brethren does so, forgetful that we are, as surely as our eighteenth- or nineteenth- or early twentieth-century forbears, creatures of a particular time and place. Earthen creatures. We forget our forms of faith and of church, accordingly, are finite.

Coming out of this formation, to conceive the theological task as imaginative construction,[10] as I was taught the task at Harvard, was to be freed to be finite. To conceive the theological task as imaginative construction allowed—indeed, required—me to acknowledge that all theological work is the work of persons in particular times and places. Our words of, to, and about God are *our* words. They are earthbound articulations; they are not eternally or everywhere adequate or authoritative.

The freedom I felt to think my own theological thoughts was accompanied by a familiar affirmation. As clear as he is about the epistemological reasons for theology as a constructive task, my teacher, Gordon Kaufman, is equally clear that theological work is work that has practical significance.[11] What we articulate with words—our earthbound articulations, this is to say—orders and orients the lives we live in the world we therewith perceive. This practical sensibility resonated with the spirit of the radical reformation traditions—Anabaptist and Radical Pietist—that had informed the Church of the Brethren's theological perspective. These traditions, and consequently the Church of the Brethren, emphasized the way one lived one's life as the test of whatever one confessed theologically.[12]

What I bodied forth in and for the world, in other words, mattered most. Here, however, theology conceived as imaginative construction could not help me. To the contrary. I worked constructively as an abstract mind. My body knew this long ago. The work of womanist and feminist theologians has helped me articulate an embodied perspective. But it has taken me until this writing to articulate what my body knows in words. To make my flesh words. Here, Judith Butler's discussion of "From Construction to Materialization," in her recent book, *Bodies That Matter,* has helped me most.[13] Judith Butler has helped me see what I had already sensed. Referring most specifically to gender construction, Butler's main point is this: "'construction' implies a culture or an agency of the social which acts upon a nature, which is itself presupposed as a passive surface, outside the social and yet its necessary counterpart."[14] The problems with this implication, as Butler makes plain, are multiple. The most compelling of these problems for me is that construction, says Butler, "misses the point that nature has a history."[15]

I see, in the light of this remark, my *body* has a history! Herein I have been *writing* my body's history. To speak instead of the sociocultural, and theological, *construction* of my body is to forget—yet again—my body is an active knower. It is to silence words made of my flesh, to tie my native tongue again. But I must also depart from Butler, since to speak, as she does, of my body in terms of "a process of materialization that stabilizes over time to produce the effect of boundary, fixity, and surface we call matter"[16] relegates my body to the realm of the productive, rent from realms of presence.

I say my body has a history which I have been writing herein as a way of clarifying my perspective on experience. During the last fifteen years or so, reference to experience has become an increasingly familiar way of speaking about one's life as a source for the theological task. I choose instead to say, "my body has a history," in order to emphasize that my experience, as all experience, is always already rendered—linguistically, symbolically, and spatially and so on—by the social and religious cultures and institutions into which I was born. So storytelling is not sufficient, save as embroidered epistemologically, since for me and for all women and men on the margins of what has been defended and defined as normative by these cultures and institutions any new articulations of experience are not unambiguous. Language itself is limited and limiting. But believing my body has a history—and that history is interpretation of experience, is meaning making—I nonetheless tell the story of my body as the location of God's revelation in my life. So doing, I disrupt the normalizing discourses into which I was born, as I accordingly "glorify God in [my] body" (I Cor. 6:20, NRSV).

I tell the story, epistemologically embroidered, understanding "body" as a textured web of physical, mental, social, affective, sexual connections with persons and places and times. John A. T. Robinson, as he distinguished the Hebraic significance of "body" from the Hellenic sense of "body" as individuation, conveys this sense of body as connectedness. He said:

> The body . . . is the symbol, not of individuality, but of solidarity. It is that which binds every individual, divinely unique. . . , in inescapable relatedness with the whole of nature and history and the totality of the cosmic order. It is the bond of continuity and unity between [human beings] and [their] environment, between individual and community, between generation and generation.[17]

But I can, after all, no more assent to Robinson's assertion that the body is symbol—I say, the body *is* solidarity—than I can to Butler's move to materialization. My body's theological knowledge is neither symbolic nor is it a proposal for the production of a form of fixity. What I know from my flesh and blood fixes me on trespass . . . for the sake of the transfiguration of my mind as well as the resurrection of my body.

I am fixed on trespass of the traditions into which I was born, traditions that link the body's finitude and mortality to the negation of women and the privilege of an abstract mind. I wrest instead a blessing from my finitude and my own mere mortality. This blessing is the clarity and courage to participate—my body a textured web—in the ongoing process of naming and renaming, of making and remaking, of binding and loosing, trusting the end to God. I am fixed on trespass as I tell the story of my body and what my body knows of death and resurrection. I am fixed on trespass as I intone a blessing on what my body knows—precisely in and of its finitude and mortality—as my words to and of and about God are made of my flesh. So doing, I celebrate my body—"a temple of the Holy Spirit within [me]" (I Cor. 6:19, NRSV), a place wherein God is pleased to reveal God's self and, indeed, to dwell.

This trespass is Gospel, Good News, to me: my body is not betrayer but friend! This Good News comes to me in the way it came to those to whom Jesus made it known: it is announced by bodies—by bodies fed and clothed and touched, by bodies freed from chains, by bodies healed. Accordingly, I believe the resurrection of the body—which, in turn, transfigures the mind—happens whenever and wherever we participate in a new solidarity with and presence to our own bodies and the bodies of others. Resurrection happens as we are incorporated into the body of the Risen One and as we honor as holy "the body of God,"[18] i.e., the earth.

But, here on Holy Saturday, I straddle days of tensive drama. I say I write to have my say in bringing hope and faith back into the world. I write to testify to my faith in God as ever-faithful Presence. I write to testify to my hope in the

Risen One who descended to the dead and then to glory. I therefore lay my body—"a temple of the Holy Spirit"—bare, trusting God may be pleased to be revealed and dwell therein. As I have written I have wrested a blessing from the anguished question with which I began: how have I forgotten my mortal body, my female body, which is my "first body of knowledge," is created to glorify God and to be "changed into the same image from glory to glory" (II Cor. 3:18)? I am created, I can now confess, not to be or become worthy but to be and become thanksgiving to God.

But I still wrestle. I wrestle with a question which will not let *me* go: "Are you the one who is to come, or shall we look for another?" (Luke 7:19, NRSV). The Lukan passage in which this text is found is itself set amid days of tensive drama. In the passage we meet John the Baptist, prophet of Advent anticipation. It was John who echoed the prophet Isaiah: "The voice of one crying in the wilderness: Prepare the way of the Lord . . . and all flesh shall see the salvation of God" (Luke 3: 4b, 6). It was John who filled people's hearts with expectation as he foretold the Good News that one was coming who would baptize not only with water but with the Holy Spirit and with fire.

Now John is in prison. Still, his disciples are loyal. They see Jesus raise the son of the widow of Nain from the dead. They hear the crowd acclaiming Jesus as a great prophet and see the rippling of his reputation throughout Judea and the surrounding country. And so they go to John in prison and tell him everything they have seen and heard. Whereupon John sends two of his disciples to Jesus to ask: "Are you the one who is to come, or shall we look for another?"

The season of Advent anticipation is past. A child has been born. Jesus has been baptized, is teaching and healing. And John is still waiting. But not as he waited before. In prison, a place of precarious presence, John is waiting and watching. For Jesus had not exactly effected Messianic expectations. Waiting was converted to crisis. No doubt especially for John.

Nonetheless, John did not send his disciples to ask: "Are you the one who is to come, or have we waited in vain?" He did not send them to ask: "Are you the one who is to come, or shall we give up?" John sent his disciples to ask: "Are you the one who is to come, or shall we wait for another?" In a place of presence, precarious presence, John waited and he sent his disciples to watch with him. He sent them to see what was happening.

I wrestle to hold onto the hope and faith to which this passage testifies. I wrestle to stir up in my self the insistent vitality of this expectancy. I wrestle to live with the conviction that something *is* happening, that God *is* doing a new thing, even after the echoes of angels' songs and the solicitations of shepherds slip away under the relentlessly clear light of our world's circumstances.

I still wrestle because my body knows that presence—revelatory presence bearing within it the possibility of realization—is always precarious presence. The child born amid Advent anticipation was a refugee child for whom no hospitality was offered, a refugee child to whom Mary sang a song about upsetting, unsettling present powers and principalities. And so I still wrestle. I ask with John's disciples: "Are you the one who is to come, or shall we look for another?"

Jesus did not and does not answer the question on the terms in which it was asked. He does not give an account of his credentials. He does not offer proof of his accomplishments. He simply says of those who have been cured of diseases and plagues and evil spirits, of those who were blind and have recovered sight: "Go and tell John what you have seen and heard: the blind receive their sight, the lame walk, the lepers are cleansed, the deaf hear, the dead are raised, the poor have good news brought to them" (Luke 7:22). All these happenings were well-known signs of the expected reign of God, of the Messianic era. So Jesus sends a reply to John that echoes the prophecy of Isaiah. More than this, the words of the prophecy are proclaimed to be present reality. Flesh and word dwell together in bodies happy and healed.

But Jesus adds: "Blessed is anyone who takes no offense at me" (Luke 7:23). Cryptic words. A phrase hanging awkwardly. What did Jesus mean? His reply had confirmed John's waiting was not for naught after all. Jesus confirmed the realized presence of his expectations. Who could take offense? Who could lose confidence, as some translations render the phrase? Even more perplexing, Jesus' dangling words well-nigh anticipate people *will* take offense, lose confidence!

Only after John's disciples have departed does Jesus speak another word to the crowds of people: "What did you go out into the wilderness to look at? A reed shaken by the wind? What then did you go out to see? Someone dressed in soft robes? Look, those who put on fine clothing and live in luxury are in royal palaces. What then did you go out to see?" (Luke 7:24b–26a).

Another unsettling speech. And I try to tame my wild wanting to settle it all. Who or what, after all, did I go out to see when I set out to tell the story of my body and what it knows? Am I still tempted by soft robes and fine clothes to cover my body laid bare? Am I still in search of someone who will tell me there will be an end to the apparent endlessness of suffering? Someone who will make me comfortable, give me a guarantee of security? Someone to make promises promises about hurt and longing? Whom did I go out to see when I set out to write?

I still wrestle. To keep hope alive and heal the fracture of faith. I know my body knows well-being is never secure and settled, never predictable. My body knows possibilities of revelatory presence realized—of new life abundant—often spring amid places thought to be barren.[19] Like the child leaping in Elizabeth's womb when Mary greeted her:

And Elizabeth was filled with the Holy Spirit and now exclaimed with a loud cry, "Blessed are you among women and blessed is the fruit of your womb.

And why has this happened to me, that the mother
of my Lord comes to me? For as soon as I heard the
sound of your greeting, the child in my womb leapt
for joy. And blessed is she who believed that there
would be a fulfillment of what was spoken to her by
the Lord (Luke 1:41–45, NRSV).

Blessed is she who believed that there would be a fulfillment,
indeed.

Blessing in biblical traditions is matched by curse. Blessing
and curse. Curse and blessing. The curse of my life has been
my absence from—even abandonment of—my self, my absence from others, and from God. Even when I was with my
self or others or God, I have too seldom been present. I know
my body knows I too long have not participated in the promise
of revelatory presence realized. Too long I have taken stock in
Cold War wisdom: "Duck and cover!" I have not been the
flesh of my words.

"Blessed is she who believed that there would be a fulfillment
of what was spoken to her by the Lord." I know what my
body knows: participation in the promise of revelatory presence realized may yet be wrested from the curse of the bondage, from absence and abandonment.

Knowing what my body knows, I am freed to be a believer.
For she who believed knew that I am, that we are, or become
what I or we believe. Word become flesh become flesh become
words. Free at last. The possibility, the promise of revelatory
presence realized. My body laid bare. And so I claim "the
power to seek new ways of being in the world" and "the courage and sustenance to act where there are no charters."[20]

I will not let go. I will still wrestle to bring hope and faith
back into the world. Since I still believe angels watch and keep
us. And my body knows they do *not* fear to tread during
tensive days of drama. Tensive days of drama, when, as my
mother said in the sermon she preached about Jacob at the
Jabbok on the occasion of my ordination to the ministry in

1984, "we can no longer stay where we are but neither do we know what lies ahead of us."

I cannot predict an ending—of the world or of my mother's life or, indeed, of this testament I now offer to others and to God. But I *will* not let go. Not until God's glory and neighbors' good[21] are radiant and flourishing upon the earth our home. Not until we, each and every one of us, find places to stand on our own and places to stand together in hope and faith on holy ground. For then we, like Jacob at his Jabbok, may see God face to face and be blessed, and be a blessing, "standing toe to toe inside . . . rigorous loving."[22] And we will be the resurrection.

In the meantime, a body knows: living abundantly is always a threshold activity. In the meantime, I am singing a childhood hymn: "This is my story, this is my song, Praising my savior all the day long." I see "angels descending, bring from above, Echoes of mercy, whispers of love."[23] Who knows, in the meantime we together may draw the Spirit of Pentecost down from the sky and set the earth on fire!

Notes

Introduction

1. H. Richard Niebuhr, *The Meaning of Revelation* (New York: Macmillan Publishing Co., and London: Collier Macmillan Publishers, 1974), p. 133. Originally published in 1941.

2. Chung Hyun Kyung, *Struggle to Be the Sun Again: Introducing Asian Women's Theology* (Maryknoll: Orbis Books, 1990), p. 111.

3. For an understanding of theology as "imaginative construction," i.e., theology as an activity of deliberate and responsible imaginative construction in contrast to traditional understandings of theology as interpretation of religious doctrines or texts, see Gordon D. Kaufman, *Essay on Theological Method* (Atlanta: Scholars Press, 1975; rev. ed. 1979); *The Theological Imagination: Constructing the Concept of God* (Philadelphia: The Westminster Press, 1981), esp. chs. 1 and 10; *In Face of Mystery: A Constructive Theology* (Cambridge: Harvard University Press, 1993), esp. Part 1. For a critique of the notion of construction, arguing against its implicit assumption that there is "a culture or an agency of the social which acts upon a nature, which is itself presupposed as a passive surface," see Judith Butler, *Bodies That Matter: On the Discursive Limits of "Sex"* (New York & London: Routledge, 1993), p. 4, and following.

4. Joan M. Jensen offers an important perspective on the role of rural women in the mid-Atlantic region as trespassers of this boundary and as active shapers of new roles for themselves in public life. See her *Loosening the Bonds: Mid-Atlantic Farm Women, 1750–1850* (New Haven and London: Yale University Press, 1986).

5. See Michel Foucault, *Discipline and Punish: The Birth of the Prison*, trans. Alan Sheridan (New York: Vintage Books, 1979), in which he discusses in excruciating detail the ways in which prisoners' bodies were "caught up in a system of constraints and privations, obligations

and prohibitions" (p. 11), were, in other words, materialized. Judith Butler, in *Bodies That Matter,* has helped me see that in this system it is the "soul" that "becomes a normative and normalizing ideal according to which the body is trained, shaped, cultivated, and invested; . . . the soul is the prison of the body" (pp. 33–34). The truth of this perception will be exemplified in the pages of this book.

6. So saying, I do not intend to imply the Christian tradition is unambiguously characterized by hatred of the body. Indeed, I have long believed the doctrine of the Incarnation to be a defining characteristic of this variegated tradition. The scholarship of Caroline Walker Bynum encourages my conviction that for all the invectives against the flesh and sexuality, the body has been integral to Christian understandings of personhood. See Caroline Walker Bynum, *Holy Feast and Holy Fast: The Religious Significance of Food to Medieval Women* (Berkeley: University of California Press, 1987) and *The Resurrection of the Body in Western Christianity, 200–1336* (New York: Columbia University Press, 1995).

7. John Donne, *Devotions, Upon Emergent Occasions, Together with Death's Duel* (Ann Arbor: The University of Michigan Press, 1975), p. 7.

8. Wendell Berry, "Manifesto: The Mad Farmer Liberation Front," in *The Country of Marriage* (New York: A Harvest Book, 1973), p. 17.

9. Ibid.

10. Hans Ur von Balthasar, *Mysterium Paschale,* trans. by Aidan Nichols, O.P. (Grand Rapids: Wm. B. Eerdmans Publishing Co., 1993), p. 148. Originally published as *Theologie der Drei Tage* in 1970.

11. Wendell Berry, "Manifesto," p. 17.

12. See *Bonds of Unity: Women, Theology, and the Worldwide Church* (Atlanta: Scholars Press, 1989), esp. chs. 3 and 4.

13. So saying, I seek a language that does not succumb either to an essentialism of the body, i.e., to a view of the body as existing in a "natural" state outside of and unaffected by cultural and religious scripts and symbols, or to a constructionism relative to the body, i.e., to a view of the body as simply a passive site of social discipline and cultural control. For a discussion of the fallacies of both these perspectives, see Paula M. Cooey, *Religious Imagination and the Body: A Feminist Analysis* (New York: Oxford University Press, 1994), esp. ch. 2. See also Elizabeth Grosz, *Volatile Bodies: Toward a Corporeal Feminism* (Bloomington and Indianapolis: Indiana University Press, 1994), esp. ch. 1., for a discussion of these fallacies and feminist versions thereof.

In contrast to Cooey's consequent discussion of body as image and symbol, Grosz insists on the tangibility and corporeality of the body in a way more akin to my perspective. Still, as Grosz acknowledges, even the notion of "corporeality" must be rethought if we are to find ways of speaking and living that are not held in thrall by what have too long been mutually exclusive categories of mind and body. Here I am heartened by Caroline Walker Bynum's most recent work, which retrieves a view of the body—its frailty and fertility, its decay and death, its resurrection to glory—that may help us craft a language in which reason, feeling, physicality, etc. have utmost integrity. See Caroline Walker Bynum, *The Resurrection of the Body in Western Christianity, 200–1336.*

14. Leonardo Boff, *Ecclesiogenesis: The Base Communities Reinvent the Church,* trans. Robert R. Barr (Maryknoll, N.Y.: Orbis Books, 1986), p. 13.

15. I was born into the Church of the Brethren, which in turn was born at the confluence of Anabaptist and Radical Pietist streams in early eighteenth-century Germany. Brethren have viewed the church not as a loose association but as a close-knit community whose life together is a means of grace, and Brethren have stressed obedient discipleship, conformity to the life of early Christian communities. The practices of adult baptism by trine immersion, the washing of feet at what is known as the Love Feast, the holy kiss, simplicity of life, and nonresistant peacemaking are among the marks distinctive of the faith, life, and witness of the Brethren.

16. Audre Lorde, "Eye to Eye: Black Women, Hatred, and Anger," in *Sister Outsider: Essays and Speeches by Audre Lorde* (Freedom, California: The Crossing Press, 1984), pp. 174–75.

17. James Baldwin, *The Evidence of Things Not Seen* (New York: Holt, Rinehart and Winston, 1985), p. 43.

18. See n. 1 above.

19. See Chung Hyun Kyung, *Struggle to be the Sun Again,* p. 39, for her articulation of *"an epistomology of the broken body."* Together with Chung Hyun Kyung I challenge the boundaries and definitions of what is accepted as "knowledge," specifically theological knowledge. I do so with acute awareness that, as Elizabeth Kamarck Minnich puts it, "power is at stake here, including the most basic power of all, the power to define what and who is real, what and who is valuable, what and who *matters"* (*Transforming Knowledge* [Philadelphia: Temple University Press, 1990], p. 173).

20. Naomi R. Goldenberg, *Returning Words to Flesh: Feminism, Psychoanalysis, and the Resurrection of the Body* (Boston: Beacon Press, 1990), p. 188.

21. See Elizabeth A. Johnson, *She Who Is: The Mystery of God in Feminist Theological Discourse* (New York: Crossroad, 1992), esp. pp. 13–15.

22. Audre Lorde, "Poetry Is Not a Luxury," in *Sister Outsider: Essays and Speeches by Audre Lorde* (Freedom, California: The Crossing Press, 1984), p. 37.

23. Amos Niven Wilder, *Grace Confounding* (Philadelphia: Fortress Press, 1972), pp. ix, x.

24. Christine Downing, *Women's Mysteries: Toward a Poetics of Gender* (New York: Crossroad, 1992).

25. Ibid., pp. 34–35.

26. Here I am heartened to be in the company of other theologians such as Saint Ephrem of fourth-century Syria, who also acknowledged that the language of poetry is more appropriate than discursive language to the mystery of life and of faith. See *The Harp of the Spirit: Eighteen Poems of Saint Ephrem*, trans. Sebastian Brock (Fellowship of St. Alban and St. Sergius, 1983). I am grateful to Gary McGee, Professor of Church History at the Assemblies of God seminary in Springfield, Missouri, for introducing me to the poetic theology of Saint Ephrem.

27. I herein walk through the open door about which Elizabeth A. Johnson writes with regard to the rediscovery of the wisdom tradition. She says: "the door is open for women, largely excluded from official religious circles, to bring the trajectory of the wisdom tradition further by reflecting on their own experience of the struggle and beauty of everyday life and naming this religiously important—every bit as significant as what occurs in more explicitly sacred times and places" ("Redeeming the Name of Christ," in *Freeing Theology: The Essentials of Theology in Feminist Perspective*, ed. Catherine Mowry LaCugna [San Francisco: HarperSanFrancisco, 1993], p. 122).

28. Goldenberg, *Returning Words to Flesh*, p. 186.

Chapter 1: Living in the Light

1. Malidoma Patrice Some, *Of Water and the Spirit: Ritual, Magic, and Initiation in the Life of an African Shaman* (New York: G. P. Putnam's Sons, 1994), p. 277.

2. See Susan Griffin, *Woman and Nature: The Roaring Inside Her* (New York: Harper & Row, 1978).

3. Mary Daly says: "The Real Presence of Lusty women is Realizing Presence. It is active potency/power to create and to transform, to render present in place and time" (*Pure Lust: Elemental Feminist Philosophy* [Boston: Beacon Press, 1984], p. 149). So it was that night.

4. Thulani Davis, *1959* (New York: Harper Perennial, 1992), p. 143.

5. See, for example, Michel Foucault, *Power/Knowledge: Selected Interviews and Other Writings, 1972–1977*, trans. Colin Gordon, Leo Marshall, John Mepham, Kate Soper (New York: Pantheon Books, 1980).

6. I saw, in other words, that, although my Anabaptist and Radical Pietist forbears may have set themselves apart from the world into disciplined communities to be a witness to another way of living, they did not leave behind the coercive dynamics they decried. What other political and religious groups perpetrated as more overtly physical abuse, Anabaptists and Radical Pietists accomplished by banning. While banning as such seldom happens in these latter days, the covert character of control exercised for the sake of conformity internal to the community and nonconformity relative to the external world is no less effective.

7. See Wade Clark Roof and William McKinney, *American Mainline Religion: Its Changing Shape and Future* (New Brunswick and London: Rutgers University Press, 1987).

8. See Robert Wuthnow, *The Restructuring of American Religion: Society and Faith since World War II* (Princeton: Princeton University Press, 1988). See also Robert Wuthnow, *The Struggle for America's Soul: Evangelicals, Liberals, & Secularism* (Grand Rapids: Wm. B. Eerdmans Publishing Co., 1989). H. R. Niebuhr set forth the particular characteristics of American church life in terms of denominationalism in his *The Social Sources of Denominationalism* (New York: A Meridan Book, 1972). Originally published in 1929.

9. R. Laurence Moore, *Religious Outsiders and the Making of Americans* (Oxford: Oxford University Press, 1986), p. x.

10. Nathan O. Hatch, *The Democratization of American Christianity* (New Haven and London: Yale University Press, 1989), esp. pp. 212–14.

11. Nadine Gordimer, "Living in the Interregnum," in *The Essential Gesture: Writing, Politics & Places* (New York: Alfred A. Knopf, 1988), p. 277.

12. H. Richard Niebuhr, *The Social Sources of Denominationalism,* p. 21.

13. Ibid.

14. Ibid., p. 25.

15. See H. Richard Niebuhr, *Christ and Culture* (New York: Harper & Row, 1951), esp. ch. 3.

16. For the classic discussion of "sect" as contrasted to "church," see Ernst Troeltsch, *The Social Teachings of the Christian Churches,* vol. 1, trans. Olive Wyon (Chicago and London: University of Chicago Press, 1976), pp. 331 ff. Originally published as *Die Soziallehren der christlichen Kirchen und Gruppen* in 1911.

17. H. Richard Niebuhr, *The Social Sources of Denominationalism,* p. 282.

18. Leonardo Boff, *Ecclesiogenesis: The Base Communities Reinvent the Church,* p. 13.

19. In this same spirit, Hisako Kinukawa says of the women's flight: "to go to Galilee is not to escape the challenges of life, but to risk their lives in involvement with Jesus in the paradox of power and suffering" (*Women and Jesus in Mark: A Japanese Feminist Perspective* [Maryknoll: Orbis Books, 1994], p. 122).

20. On this point, I agree with the feminist critique that traditional theological understandings of suffering as salvific have supported, even encouraged, the epidemic of violence against women. See, for example, *Christianity, Patriarchy, and Abuse: A Feminist Critique*, eds. Joanne Carlson Brown and Carol R. Bohn (New York: Pilgrim Press, 1989) and Rita Nakashima Brock, *Journeys By Heart: A Christology of Erotic Power* (New York: Crossroad, 1988).

21. Cf. Alexandra R. Brown, *The Cross and Human Transformation: Paul's Apocalyptic Word in Corinthians* (Minneapolis: Fortress Press, 1995).

22. Montesquieu, according to Hannah Arendt, said "the outstanding characteristic of tyranny was that it rested on isolation—on the tyrant from his subjects and the isolation of the subjects from each other through mutual fear and suspicion—and hence that tyranny was not one form of government among others but contradicted the essential human condition of plurality, the acting and speaking together, which is the condition of all forms of political organization" (Hannah Arendt, *The Human Condition: A Study of the Central Dilemmas Facing Modern Man* [Garden City: Doubleday & Co., 1959], p. 181). What I now realize is that my confinement, and accordingly my collaboration, were carried out in the name of community. Yet, precisely "the essential human condition of plurality, the acting and speaking together" was absent, abrogated. I saw that in these instances having to do with charges of sexual harassment, as in so many others, privatization not publicity, division not discussion, separation not support, were the fetters that formed our thralldom. All the while, tyranny thrived amid plays for power and ploys about perfection and purity.

23. "O Love That Wilt Not Let Me Go," *The Brethren Hymnal* (Elgin, Illinois: House of the Church of the Brethren, 1951), no. 271.

24. Ibid., no. 349.

25. Mark Juergensmeyer, *The New Cold War? Religious Nationalism Confronts the Secular State* (Berkeley: University of California Press, 1993).

26. Ibid., p. 157.

27. I do not view these communities, as does Lewis Mudge in *The Sense of a People: Toward a Church for a Human Future*, as "contempo-

rary renewal communities" ([Philadelphia: Trinity Press, International, 1992], p. 86), but as themselves ecclesial realities.

28. See, for example, Leonardo Boff, *Ecclesiogenesis: The Base Communities Reinvent the Church.*

29. See, for example, Lamin Sanneh, *West African Christianity: The Religious Impact* (Maryknoll, New York: Orbis Books, 1983).

30. See, for example, Robert Wuthnow, *Sharing the Journey: Support Groups and America's New Quest for Community* (New York: The Free Press, 1994). See also Roberta Bondi, "House Churches and Alternative Communities Within the Church," *Mid-Stream: The Ecumenical Movement Today,* vol. 33, no. 4 (October 1994):435–41.

31. See, for example, *We Dare to Dream: Doing Theology as Asian Women,* eds. Virginia Fabella M. M. and Sun Ai Lee Park (Hong Kong: Asian Women's Resource Center for Culture and Theology and The EATWOT Women's Commission in Asia, 1989).

32. See, for example, Rosemary Radford Ruether, *Women-Church: Theology & Practice of Feminist Liturgical Communities* (New York: Harper & Row, 1985); Elisabeth Schussler Fiorenza, *Discipleship of Equals: A Critical Feminist Ekklesialogy of Liberation* (New York: Crossroad, 1993); Letty M. Russell, *Church in the Round: Feminist Interpretation of the Church* (Philadelphia: The Westminster Press, 1993).

33. Here too I know, as Julia Kristeva has reminded me, that "'word' and 'flesh' can meet at any moment, for better or for worse" (*In the Beginning Was Love: Psychoanalysis and Faith,* trans. by Arthur Goldhammer [New York: Columbia University Press, 1987], p. 6).

34. See *"Lumen Gentium,"* in *The Documents of Vatican II,* ed. Walter M. Abbott, S. J. (New York: Guild Press/America Press/Association Press, 1966), pp. 14 ff.

35. Walbert Buhlmann, *With Eyes to See: Church and World in the Third Millennium,* trans. by Robert R. Barr (Middlegreen, Slough, United Kingdom: St. Paul Publications, 1990), p. 151. Buhlmann does go on to distinguish sacramental and nonsacramental arenas of church life, reserving power in the former for church officials while granting "plenary authority" to all disciples in the latter (pp. 151–52). For an understanding of the church wherein this "plenary authority" extends to the entire life of the church, see Lewis S. Mudge, *The Sense of a People: Toward a Church for the Human Future.*

36. See John Zizioulas, *Being as Communion: Studies in Personhood and the Church* (Crestwood, New York: St. Vladimir's Seminary Press, 1985), for a discussion of both communion and personhood in ecclesiological perspective.

37. See, for example, Leonid Ouspensky, "The Meaning and Language of Icons," in *The Meaning of Icons*, Leonid Ouspensky and Vladimir Lossky, eds. (Crestwood, New York: St. Vladimir's Seminary Press, 1982), esp. pp. 34–35. Ouspensky refers to Philaret, Metropolitan of Moscow and Kolomna, St. Gregory Palamas, and St. Simeon the New Theologian in this regard. See also Ouspensky, *Theology of the Icon* (Crestwood, New York: St. Vladimir's Seminary Press, 1978).

38. In the words of *"Lumen Gentium,"* words that echo Cardinal Newman's notion of the "sense of the faithful:" "The body of the faithful as a whole, anointed as they are by the Holy One (cf. John 2:20, 27), cannot err in matters of belief. Thanks to a supernatural sense of the faith, which characterizes the People as a whole, it manifests this unerring quality when, 'from the bishops down to the last member of the laity,' it shows universal agreement in matters of faith and morals" (*The Documents of Vatican II*, p. 29).

39. I am indebted to Michael Dyson, professor at Brown University, for this insight on the occasion of his preaching in the Divinity School chapel in Rochester, New York, in March, 1994.

40. Cited by Virginia Ramey Mollenkott, *Sensuous Spirituality: Out from Fundamentalism* (New York: Crossroad, 1992), p. 72.

Chapter 2: A Heart for Hospitality

1. James Baldwin, *The Evidence of Things Not Seen* (New York: Holt, Rinehart and Winston, 1985), p. 101.

2. Audre Lorde, *The Cancer Journals* (San Francisco: spinsters/aunt lute, 1980), pp. 27–28.

3. Ibid., p. 20.

4. J. M. Coetzee, *Age of Iron* (New York: Random House, 1990), p. 112.

5. Ibid.

6. F. Luis de Granada, *Guida de pecadores*, cited by Jean Delumeau, *Sin and Fear: The Emergence of a Western Guilt Culture 13th–18th Centuries*, trans. Eric Nicholson (New York: St. Martin's Press, 1990), p. 25.

7. Self-sacrificial love is a feature not only of radical reformation traditions. The understanding that self-sacrificial love is the highest form of love—agape love—is part of monastic, mystic, and many theologies of magisterial Protestant traditions as well. For a summary of some of these streams of thought about self-sacrificial love, see Daniel Day Williams, *The Spirit and the Forms of Love* (Washington, D.C.: University Press of America, 1981), esp. pp. 192 ff. What distinguishes the radical reformation tradition in this regard is a relative absence of abundant grace through which the self may grow into its own full stature.

8. "Praise to the Lord, the Almighty," *The Brethren Hymnal* (Elgin, Illinois: House of the Church of the Brethren, 1951) #37. I recently sang this hymn from the hymnal of the Episcopal Church, and was startled to find that this phrase is rendered "*who* with his love doth befriend thee!" A remarkable difference revealing the remarkable graciousness of God's love, a graciousness I glimpse now and again, more and more often.

9. Ibid., p. 4.

10. Ibid., p. 189.

11. Ibid., p. 196.

12. Ibid., pp. 136–37.

13. I agree with ecumenical colleagues at the Institute for Ecumenical Research in Strasbourg, France, that, in talking of a "crisis of the ecumenical movement," "both trivialization and dramatization must be avoided" (*Crisis and Challenge of the Ecumenical Movement: Integrity and Indivisibility* [Geneva: WCC Publications, 1994], p. 1).

14. This vision has been most fully embodied in the sixty or so united churches, in all continental regions of the world, that have come into being in the past 175 years. Examples of these united churches are the Church of North India, the United Reformed Church in the United Kingdom, the United Church of Christ in Zaire, the United Church of Christ in the Philippines.

15. Syncretism came into the ecumenical vocabulary as a word with a negative meaning at the meeting of the International Missionary Council at Tambaram, South India, in 1938. It was Hendrik Kraemer, a devoted Barthian, who defined "syncretism" as "illegitimate mingling of different religious elements" in his *Christian Message in a Non-Christian World*, the conference study book [London: Edinburgh House, 1947], p. 203). Most recently, the word was spoken, more negatively than ever, in judgment of the presentation by Professor Chung Hyun Kyung of Korea at the Seventh Assembly of the World Council of Churches. See "Come, Holy Spirit—Renew the Whole Creation," in *Signs of the Spirit: Official Report, Seventh Assembly, Canberra, Australia, 7–20 February 1991*, ed. Michael Kinnamon (Geneva: WCC Publications/Grand Rapids: Wm. B. Eerdmans, 1991), pp. 37 ff. To this event and the consequent controversy we will return later in this chapter.

16. This debate is at least as old as the exchange between biblical scholars Raymond Brown and Ernst Kaesemann at the Fourth World Conference on Faith and Order. See *The Fourth World Conference on Faith and Order, Montreal 1963*, ed. P. C. Rodger and L. Vischer. Faith and Order Paper No. 42 (London: S.C.M. Press, 1964). See also Brown, "The Unity and Diversity in New Testament Ecclesiology," *Novum Tes-*

tamentum 6 (1963):302–3 and Kaesemann, "Unity and Diversity in New Testament Ecclesiology," *Novum Testamentum* 6 (1963):290.

17. For my understanding of conversation, see my *Bonds of Unity: Women, Theology and the Worldwide Church*, pp. 169 ff.

18. One of the earliest discussions of the limits of acceptable diversity, as the terms are presently being used, is by Michael Kinnamon in *Truth and Community: Diversity and Its Limits in the Ecumenical Movement* (Grand Rapids: Wm. B. Eerdmans/Geneva: World Council of Churches, 1988). Kinnamon reminds us that the search for unity has always been held together with the search, or "spiritual battle," as Willem Visser't Hooft put it in "Pluralism—Temptation or Opportunity?" (*The Ecumenical Review* [April 1966]:147), for truth. Kinnamon cites the ecumenical conviction that apartheid is heresy as an example of the understanding that not all diversity—politically or theologically—is acceptable insofar as truth and error are also always at stake. In conclusion, Kinnamon offers two principles by which the limits of acceptable diversity may be discerned: the absence of love and idolatry (pp. 111 ff.).

19. See "Come, Holy Spirit—Renew the Whole Creation," in *Signs of the Spirit*, pp. 38–39.

20. Ibid., p. 39. For a fuller understanding of *Han*, see Chung Hyun Kyung, *Struggle to Be the Sun Again: Introducing Asian Women's Theology*, esp. p. 23. See also Andrew Sung Park, *The Wounded Heart of God: The Asian Concept of Han and the Christian Doctrine of Sin* (Nashville: Abingdon Press, 1993).

21. "Canberra 1991: A Personal Overview and Introduction," in *Signs of the Spirit*, pp. 15–16.

22. Ibid., p. 16.

23. Here it is significant to note that the twentieth-century ecumenical movement emerged at the great world missionary conference in Edinburgh in 1910. Those present were acutely aware that their missionary work, their proclamation of the Gospel of love, etc., was seriously undercut by continuing divisions and even conflicts on the fields of mission. For an overview of this era, see *A History of the Ecumenical Movement, 1517–1948*, eds. Ruth Rouse and Stephen Neill (Geneva: World Council of Churches, 1986).

24. In speaking of embrace relative to community, I take exception to Parker Palmer who says communities are usually created by acts of exclusion, i.e., by deciding who is in and who is out (*The Company of Strangers: Christians and the Renewal of American Public Life* [New York: Crossroad, 1983], p. 130.

25. See Genesis 18:1 ff.

26. See Hebrews 13:2.

27. Letty M. Russell, *Church in the Round: Feminist Interpretation of the Church* (Philadelphia: The Westminster Press, 1993), p. 179.

28. Ibid., p. 173.

29. Ibid. See also Thomas Ogletree, *Hospitality to the Stranger: Dimensions of Moral Understanding* (Philadelphia: Fortress Press, 1985).

30. Ibid. See John Koenig, *New Testament Hospitality: Partnership with Strangers as Promise and Mission* (Philadelphia: Fortress Press, 1985), p. 8.

31. For my understanding of relinquishment, see my *Bonds of Unity: Women, Theology and the Worldwide Church*, p. 170 and p. 174, notes 14 and 15. In short, I do not believe relinquishment is "simply the subordination or subjugation or surrender of one to another. It is a moment of offering . . . In the moment of relinquishment, I choose to participate with others, rather than to make predictions about a new creation" (p. 170).
Herein I deepen my earlier understanding inasmuch as I believe relinquishment is integrally connected to risk of *being* chosen, not simply choosing to participate with others.

32. Quoted by Mary Tanner, "Ordination of Women," in *Dictionary of the Ecumenical Movement*, eds. Nicholas Lossky, Jose Miguez Bonino, John S. Pobee, Tom F. Stransky, Geoffrey Wainwright, Pauline Webb (Geneva: WCC Publications/Grand Rapids: William B. Eerdmans Publishing, 1991), p. 753.

33. "Ordinatio Sacerdotalils," *National Catholic Reporter*, Vol. 30, No. 32 (June 17, 1994), p. 7.

34. Julia Kristeva, *Strangers to Ourselves*, trans. Leon S. Roudiez (New York: Columbia University Press, 1991).

35. Audre Lorde, *A Burst of Light* (Ithaca, New York: Firebrand Books, 1988), pp. 117–18.

36. Leonardo Boff, *Trinity and Society*, trans. Paul Burns (Maryknoll, New York: Orbis Books, 1988), p. 144.

37. Ibid., p. 148.

38. Ibid., p. 148.

39. Ibid., pp. 148–49.

40. Konrad Raiser, General Secretary of the World Council of Churches, makes a similar point about the monistic structure of unity thinking that has predominated in the ecumenical paradigm. In sketching a way ahead, he draws upon the social doctrine of the Trinity found in the Greek fathers, which contrasts to the Latin tradition's preoccupation with relating divine unity to the divine Trinity, preoccupation already portending contemporary debates about unity and diversity. See *Ecu-*

menism in Transition: A Paradigm Shift in the Ecumenical Movement?* (Geneva: WCC Publications, 1991), esp. pp. 93 ff.

41. Groupe des Dombes, For the Conversion of the Churches, trans. James Greig (Geneva: WCC Publications, 1993).

42. Ibid., p. 20.

43. Ibid., p. 78.

Chapter 3: The Promise of Presence

1. William Styron, Darkness Visible: A Memoir of Madness (New York: Random House, 1990), p. 62.

2. Jeffrey L. Geller and Maxine Harris, Women of the Asylum: Voices from Behind the Walls, 1840–1945 (New York: Doubleday, Anchor Books, 1994), pp. 8, 9. See also Phyllis Chesler, Women and Madness (San Diego: Harcourt Brace Jovanovich, A Harvest/HBJ Book, reprint, 1989), for a classic statement of these matters; and Elizabeth Lunbeck, The Psychiatric Persuasion: Knowledge, Gender, and Power in Modern America (Princeton: Princeton University Press, 1994), for a fascinating study of the ideas of gender that have informed an emerging "psychiatry of the normal."

3. Stephanie Golden, The Women Outside: Meanings and Myths of Homelessness (Berkeley: University of California Press, 1992), p. 174.

4. See Michel Foucault, Madness and Civilization: A History of Insanity in the Age of Reason, trans. Richard Howard (New York: Random House, Vintage Books, 1973) for an analysis of the exile of unreason and the exile of mad people from society, as well as of the identification of reason with the rule of the Father.

5. Paul Ricoeur, "The Critique of Religion," in The Philosophy of Paul Recoeur: An Anthology of His Work, eds. Charles E. Reagan & David Stewart (Boston: Beacon Press, 1978), p. 217.

6. Ibid., p. 237.

7. Brita Gill, "A Ministry of Presence," in Women Ministers: How Women are Redefining Traditional Roles, ed. Judith L. Weidman (San Francisco: Harper & Row, Publishers, 1981).

8. Ibid., p. 91.

9. Ibid.

10. Ibid., p. 92.

11. Ralph Harper, On Presence: Variations and Reflections (Philadelphia: Trinity Press International, 1991), pp. 4, 7.

12. Kathleen B. Jones, "On Authority: Or, Why Women Are Not Entitled to Speak," in Feminism and Foucault: Reflections on Resistance, eds. Irene Diamond and Lee Quinby (Boston: Northeastern University, 1988).

13. Ibid., pp. 119–20.

14. Ibid., p. 120.

15. Ibid.

16. Ibid.

17. Ibid.

18. Ibid., p. 125.

19. Ibid., p. 127.

20. See Hannah Arendt, "What Is Authority?" in *Between Past and Future: Eight Exercises in Political Thought* (New York: Penguin Books, 1954), pp. 121–23.

21. Ibid., p. 126.

22. Ibid., p. 128.

23. Ibid.

24. Letty M. Russell, *Household of Freedom: Authority in Feminist Theology* (Philadelphia: The Westminster Press, 1987).

25. Ibid., pp. 93, 92.

26. Ibid., pp. 96 ff.

27. Victoria Lee Erickson, *Where Silence Speaks: Feminism, Social Theory, and Religion* (Minneapolis: Fortress Press, 1993), p. 97.

28. See John E. Thiel, *Imagination and Authority: Theological Authorship in the Modern Tradition* (Minneapolis: Fortress Press, 1991).

29. Carter Heyward, *Touching Our Strength: The Erotic as Power and the Love of God* (San Francisco: Harper & Row, Publishers, 1989), p. 97.

30. Hannah Arendt, "Tradition and the Modern Age," in *Between Past and Future*, p. 26.

31. Christa Wolf, source unknown. Cf. Andreas Huyssen, *Twilight Memories: Marking Time in a Culture of Amnesia* (New York and London: Routledge, 1995).

32. Mercy Amba Oduyoye, "Be a Woman, and Africa Will Be Strong," in *Inheriting Our Mothers' Gardens: Feminist Theology in Third World Perspective*, eds. Letty M. Russell et al. (Philadelphia: The Westminster Press, 1988), p. 49.

33. Ibid.

34. See Naomi Wolf, *Fire with Fire: The New Female Power and How It Will Change the 21st Century* (New York: Random House, 1993), esp. ch. 10, for a compelling, if controversial, discussion of what she calls "victim feminism." Cf. Katie Roiphe, *The Morning After: Sex, Fear, and Feminism on Campus* (Boston: Little, Brown and Co., 1993).

35. T. Obinkaram Echewa, *I Saw the Sky Catch Fire* (New York: Penguin Books, A Plume Book, 1993).

36. Ibid., p. 38.

37. Ibid., pp. 38–39.

38. Ibid., p. 39.
39. Ibid., p. 172.
40. Ibid., p. 198.
41. Ibid., p. 204.
42. Ibid.
43. Ibid., p. 208.
44. Ibid.
45. Ibid.
46. Ibid.

Chapter 4: Telling the Truth

1. Dorothy Allison, *Skin: Talking About Sex, Class & Literature* (Ithaca, New York: Firebrand Books, 1994), pp. 250–51.

2. See Susan Griffin, *Women and Nature: The Roaring Inside* (New York: Harper & Row, 1978).

3. Audre Lorde, *The Cancer Journals* (San Francisco: spinsters/aunt lute, 1980), p. 20.

4. For an excellent, and chilling, exploration of the witch-hunts and their lessons for these days of backlash, see Anne Llewellyn Barstow, *Witchcraze: A New History of the European Witch Hunts* (San Francisco: HarperCollins, A Pandora Book, 1994). See also Stephanie Golden, *The Women Outside: Meanings and Myths of Homelessness* (Berkeley: University of California Press, 1992), esp. chs. 3 and 5.

5. Virginia Ramey Mollenkott, *Sensuous Spirituality: Out from Fundamentalism*, pp. 159 ff.

6. See Elizabeth A. Johnson, *She Who Is: The Mystery of God in Feminist Theological Discourse* (New York: Crossroad, 1992), esp. pp. 13 ff.

7. I refer the reader to John J. McNeill's classic, *The Church and the Homosexual* (Boston: Beacon Press, 4th ed., 1993) and to his most recent, *Freedom, Glorious Freedom: The Spiritual Journey to the Fullness of Life for Gays, Lesbians, and Everybody Else* (Boston: Beacon Press, 1995); to John Boswell's, *Christianity, Social Tolerance, and Homosexuality: Gay People in Western Europe from the Beginning of the Christian Era to the Fourteenth Century* (Chicago: University of Chicago Press, 1980); to Virginia Ramey Mollenkott's *Sensuous Spirituality: Out from Fundamentalism*, for what I find the finest considerations of these issues and debates. For a careful comparative and critical reading of recent U.S. church policy statements on sexuality, specifically homosexuality, that intends to stake out common ground for conversation, see Mark Ellingsen, "Homosexuality and the Churches: A Quest for the Nicene Vision,"

Journal of Ecumenical Studies, vol. 30, nos. 3–4 (Summer–Fall, 1993):354–71.

8. Here I recall the two principles Michael Kinnamon offers, principles by which the limits of acceptable diversity may be discerned: the absence of love and idolatry (*Truth and Community: Diversity and Its Limits in the Ecumenical Movement*, pp. 111 ff). Truth does not flourish where love does not flourish, as the biblical injunction about telling the truth in love also suggests.

9. Chung Hyun Kyung, *Struggle to Be the Sun Again: Introducing Asian Women's Theology*, p. 111.

10. Parker Palmer, *To Know as We Are Known: A Spirituality of Education* (San Francisco: Harper & Row, Publishers, 1983), p. 48.

11. Ibid., p. 49.

12. See Loyal Rue, *By the Grace of Guile: The Role of Deception in Natural History and Human Affairs* (Oxford: Oxford University Press, 1994).

13. Dorothy Allison, *Skin*, p. 250.

14. James Baldwin, *The Evidence of Things Not Seen*, p. 43.

15. J. M. Coetzee, *Age of Iron*, p. 106.

16. Walker Percy, "The Message in the Bottle," in *The Message in the Bottle: How Queer Man Is, How Queer Language Is, and What One Has to Do with the Other* (New York: Farrar, Straus and Giroux, 1977), p. 144.

17. Paul Ricoeur, "The Critique of Religion," in *The Philosophy of Paul Ricoeur: An Anthology of His Work*, eds. Charles E. Reagan & David Stewart (Boston: Beacon Press, 1978), p. 219. See also, for example, Karl Barth, "The Strange New World within the Bible," in *The Word of God and the Word of Man*, trans. Douglas Horton (New York: Harper & Row, Publishers, 1957). Originally an address delivered in 1916.

18. Hannah Arendt, *The Human Condition: A Study of the Central Dilemmas Facing Modern Man*, p. 160.

19. H. Richard Niebuhr, *The Meaning of Revelation*, p. 95.

20. Kate Braverman, *Palm Latitudes* (New York: Penguin Books, A Viking Book, 1988), p. 197.

21. Harriette Arnow, *The Dollmaker*. The Southern Writers Series (New York: Avon Books, 1972), p. 440. Originally published in 1954.

22. Arendt, *The Human Condition*, p. 160.

23. Naomi R. Goldenberg, *Returning Words to Flesh: Feminism, Psychoanalysis, and the Resurrection of the Body*, p. 188.

Chapter 5: God's Glory and Neighbors' Good

1. Walker Percy, *The Thanatos Syndrome* (New York: Farrar, Straus and Giroux, 1987), p. 365.

2. See Nadine Gordimer, "Living in the Interregnum," in *The Essential Gesture: Writing, Politics & Places*. Cf. *Selections from the Prison Notebooks of Antonio Gramsci*, eds. Quintin Hoare and Geoffrey Nowell Smith (London: Lawrence & Wishart, 1971).

3. Nadine Gordimer, "Living in the Interregnum," *The Essential Gesture: Writing, Politics & Places*, p. 263.

4. Ibid., p. 264.

5. See Rudolf Otto, *The Idea of the Holy* (Oxford: Oxford University Press, 1977). Originally published in 1923.

6. See Ernst Troeltsch, *The Social Teachings of the Christian Churches*, vol. I, pp. 331 ff.

7. For a discussion of the sectarian and ecumenical streams as they have flowed together, see Donald F. Durnbaugh, *The Believers' Church: The History and Character of Radical Protestantism* (New York: The Macmillan Co. and London: Collier-Macmillan Ltd., 1968), esp. ch. 12.

8. See chapter 2, pp. 43–44. See also Parker Palmer, *The Company of Strangers: Christians and the Renewal of American Public Life*, p. 130.

9. See my "Now Is the Time So Urgent: Called into God's Future," in *Brethren In Transition: 20th Century Directions and Dilemmas*, ed. Emmet F. Bittinger (Camden, Maine: Penobscot Press, 1992), pp. 221 ff.

10. See Gordon D. Kaufman, *An Essay on Theological Method* and *In Face of Mystery: A Constructive Theology*, esp. Pt. 1.

11. In keeping with his Kantian epistemology, Gordon Kaufman emphasizes that the criterion for truth claims is practical not speculative. Accordingly, Kaufman is more concerned with asking how we order and orient our lives than with asking what we can know or how we are to live per se, since these latter two questions imply a reality outside ourselves by which such questions could be answered absolutely.

12. It is in this sense that I have always thought Gordon Kaufman, for all his classically apologetic and constructive theological work with regard to the wider culture, is at heart a Mennonite theologian. I am convinced, this is to say, his ethical convictions have formed his epistemology, rather than the reverse as is so often reckoned.

13. See Judith Butler, *Bodies That Matter: On the Discursive Limits of "Sex,"* pp. 4 ff.

14. Ibid., p. 4.

15. Ibid., p. 5.

16. Ibid.

17. John A. T. Robinson, *In the End, God . . . : A Study of the Christian Doctrine of the Last Things* (London: James Clarke & Co., Ltd., 1950), pp. 86–87.

18. See Sallie McFague, *The Body of God: An Ecological Theology* (Minneapolis: Fortress Press, 1993).

19. Hannah Arendt, in *The Human Condition*, speaks of "natality" as "the miracle that saves the world, the realm of human affairs, from its normal, 'natural' ruin." The birth of new persons disrupts what is, disrupts in ways that are predictably unpredictable, says Arendt. Precisely therefore, "natality" introduces new possibilities. And, says Arendt: "It is this faith in and hope for the world that found its most glorious and succinct expression in the few words with which the Gospels announced their 'glad tidings': 'A child has been born unto us,'" (*The Human Condition: A Study of the Central Dilemmas Facing Modern Man*, p. 247).

20. Audre Lorde, "The Master's Tools Will Never Dismantle the Master's House," in *Sister Outsider: Essays and Speeches by Audre Lorde*, p. 111.

21. This phrase is the motto on the seal of Alexander Mack, founder and first minister of the Church of the Brethren.

22. Audre Lorde, "Eye to Eye: Black Women, Hatred, and Anger, in *Sister Outsider*, p. 175.

23. "Blessed Assurance, Jesus Is Mine," *The Brethren Hymnal* (Elgin: House of the Church of the Brethren, 1951), no. 436.

Index